Praise for *My Mother and Other Secrets*

'I devoured this in 24 hours . . . such is the quality and style of Wendyl's personal writing. A true memoir that is emotive, thoughtful and considered . . . It's a powerful story of a daughter's love and commitment to seek the best for her mother's care . . . makes for a truthful memoir that I could not draw away from.'

Sue Reid, Paper Plus

'A genealogical detective story of sorts . . . told with Nissen's usual journalistic precision and insight.'

Caroline Barron, *Sunday Star-Times*

'*My Mother and Other Secrets* is not a book of grievance nor is it a misery memoir. It's a book of understanding. More so, it's a book propelled by the redeeming power of stories . . . Nissen tells her family's story with insight and good humour . . . wise, well-told, sympathetic, and highly readable.'

Steve Braunias, *Newsroom*

'Wendyl Nissen knows how to grab readers with a first sentence . . . compelling . . . frank and often moving.'

Elspeth McLean, *Otago Daily Times*

'Very raw material in the hands of a seasoned storyteller.'

***Sunday* magazine**

My mother
and other secrets

Wendyl Nissen

ALLEN&UNWIN
SYDNEY · MELBOURNE · AUCKLAND · LONDON

First published in 2021.
This edition published in 2022.

Allen & Unwin
Level 2, 10 College Hill, Freemans Bay
Auckland 1011, New Zealand
Phone: (64 9) 377 3800
Email: auckland@allenandunwin.com
Web: www.allenandunwin.co.nz

83 Alexander Street
Crows Nest NSW 2065, Australia
Phone: (61 2) 8425 0100

A catalogue record for this book is available from
the National Library of New Zealand.

ISBN 978 1 76106 645 0

Design by Madeleine Kane
Set in Adobe Caslon Pro
Printed and bound in Australia by SOS Print + Media Group

1 3 5 7 9 10 8 6 4 2

To my parents, Elis and Cedric

Contents

Introduction

When I started writing this book it was a simple memoir of my mother's interesting life and a guide for people dealing with dementia. What I hadn't counted on was the number of secrets my family held, on both sides. Wild tales and stories of intrigue took me over, and before I knew it I was uncovering, and then writing, a family history my parents had not been aware of — or, perhaps, had not wanted to know.

This is also a book about how women suffer, especially in my mother's era, when childhoods were tough, and when women had to fight for every bit of independence they gained, if they gained any at all. It was a time when mental illness was stigmatised, so you just got on with it and did the best you could. I know that my mother would take pills and then sleep for a long time to escape what was going on in her head. I know she drank alcohol to help get away from it all. I don't blame her. I don't have voices in my head or dark moods. Or the impulse to abuse my children verbally and physically. But if I did, I think I would want to take something to make me sleep and escape for long periods quite a lot.

My mother could be cruel and unkind to me, but it was what she knew and what she had been taught and what her brain was doing to her. She could also be extraordinarily nice to many people. Inclusive, warm, generous and lovely. I know that she did the best she could with her life, made it a good one and I'm proud of her for that.

• • •

Following Mum's death I embarked on a research project which I expected to be quite short. I had submitted her DNA to Ancestry.com several years earlier, simply to find out whether I could find her birth father, as she had been adopted out as a baby. I had suggested finding him to my mother several times when she was alive, but always got a negative reaction. She simply wasn't interested, and when I found out more about him I would understand why. I was given the firm impression that I was welcome to do the research but she would prefer that she wasn't around to hear about it. In other words, do it after her death. I'm also pretty sure she knew there would be more to uncover than just the name of her father, hence her reluctance.

When I started the research I found myself going down rabbit holes that I never expected to be there, and ended up exploring leads and tunnels of research that told me stories I had never heard or even suspected the existence of. I unearthed relatives I never knew about, and this helped me understand my mother properly, for the first time. She was a complex woman from a complex background. I'm a journalist, so uncovering secrets is something I love to do. For me, the research path that takes you down rabbit holes and brings you up somewhere totally unexpected is a thrill. Which is why this book took over my life in a lovely, all-consuming way. When I finally finished tying up all the leads and writing them down in this book, my husband joked: 'I always knew you were descended from rogues and scoundrels.'

My parents were born to a generation that kept secrets. Big secrets for a long time, and usually they took them to their graves. Their parents' generation had lived through two world wars and a depression, and suffered a lot of deprivation. I can understand why they were reluctant to sit around on a Sunday afternoon and share it all over a cup of tea. My parents' generation wasn't much better as they ventured into new lives, new prosperity, and a new social level which meant that you didn't really want to be telling people about the sins of your fathers. You would rather they didn't know the sordid secrets of your past.

I found out that my parents knew very little about their parents or grandparents and saw no reason to explore further. They both knew there were things they didn't really know about — sins and suffering — and they were quite happy to keep it that way. Then I decided to write this book, which has exposed secrets and stories that I found fascinating; it's a cliché, but I was able to weave a tapestry of my existence using the threads of research. The process, the completed job — this book — helped me become a little more whole. I now knew what came before. I think that is very healthy for the mind; it certainly was for mine.

After sitting back in wonder at something my computer had thrown up, I would often pause to consider what my mother would have said if she were alive to hear the latest detail. She most likely would have looked at me, laughed, and then said, 'Is that right? Well I never!' Then she would have clamped her mouth tight shut so as not to let out any more secrets that had been long buried.

Dad had the fortune, or possibly misfortune, to be alive to hear these secrets. Sometimes he shed a tear at the information I found out about his father and mother; other times he just shook his head and said, 'I had no idea. Thank you.' And that was it.

As a result of all my digging I developed a strong connection with my paternal grandfather, Arthur, who I never knew, and my maternal adopted grandmother, Olive, who I have no memory of as I only met her as a baby. I started talking to them in my mind and acknowledging their pain. I found and visited Arthur's grave for the first time, and did the same with Olive. It felt great to have those two people in my heart at last.

• • •

There were two children in our immediate family and I'm only going to tell the story from the perspective of one of them. I've done my best to leave my brother Mark out of this story because he has his own version of what happened to us and his own story to tell.

My father, Cedric, is still alive and has given me permission to write this book, as did my mother when she was alive. I've done my best to be truthful and respect his dignity as well.

It is hard to write about your family when the subject matter is difficult. I once bravely put my hand up at a reading in the Auckland Town Hall and asked celebrated American writer David Sedaris how his family reacted when he wrote so much about them, often in unflattering ways. His answer was simple: 'Whenever I write about someone in my family, I give it to them first. And I say, "Is there anything you want me to change or get rid of?" You can portray them with real flaws and depth without betraying them.'

My dad has been given this opportunity.

CHAPTER 1

Needles

O n the day I killed my mother I sewed a dress. It was the first dress I had sewn in nearly 40 years, and I was a bit rusty. I had bought the material online: a fine black netting fabric, beautifully embroidered with flowers, along with a very simple pattern that I hoped would be flattering. A simple, straight shift dress with elbow-length sleeves where I allowed a brief flutter of ruched fabric to give the sleeves a little extra something. I'd remembered how to pin the delicate tissue paper of the pattern onto the fabric, making sure I knew the fabric's wrong and right sides. I had carefully cut each piece out with pinking shears and then pinned the darts.

It was still early because I had woken at 5.30 a.m. I sometimes do this and simply make a cup of tea and have a chat with my husband, Paul, who is always awake at that time reading a book or working on his laptop. But he was in Auckland for work, and I was alone in our Hokianga home. It was the middle of winter and still dark outside. I made a pot of tea and drew the curtains in the bedroom so that I could see the sun when it came up. I hopped back into bed and sipped the tea, thinking about the day ahead. It was Saturday, technically a day off, but I write something most days — so would it be work writing or fun writing? I was in the middle of writing my book *A Natural Year* and I was enjoying it. I would probably do some of that.

Then I remembered the fabric, the pattern, the pins with their delicious pearl bobbles at the end, and the sewing machine I had set up the night before on our old kauri dining table. I might as well get started.

Sewing was a big part of my childhood. In the '70s it was cheaper to sew your own clothes than buy them from boutiques or department stores like Farmers, George Court's, Rendells or Smith and Caughey's. Our family was always on a budget, so I grew up wearing dresses my mother had sewn on her trusty white Elna machine. I had also grown up knowing that when Mum was sewing it was best to make yourself scarce. She didn't enjoy sewing and would often fly into a rage as she battled to get a zip in straight.

When I became a teenager and had been taught how to sew by my mum and in my school's home economics classes, I began sewing my own clothes. Mum would give me the universal family benefit money she received for me — about $12 a week from memory — and the deal was that I would sew all my own clothes, with the exception of undies and a pair of jeans, which are fairly impossible to sew yourself. I loved creating one-off pieces and the process of riding down to the local haberdasher's on my bike, where I would pore over the huge Simplicity, Butterick and Vogue pattern catalogues before selecting a pattern in my size, then choosing the fabric to go with it.

One weekend I was eagerly sewing a new dress to wear to a party that night. I was fifteen and had a real talent for making great-looking clothes, even if I say so myself. I was sewing on the Elna out in the lounge, my preferred area for creating things, when my mother and I had a disagreement. I can't remember what it was about but I probably answered her back. That was my main offence in my teen years. I was good at answering back, and still am.

My mother immediately confiscated her sewing machine from me as punishment. She had the knack of finding the most annoying punishments and she knew that this one was a good one. No sewing machine meant no dress for my party that night.

At that time I had a part-time job at the local chemist on Friday nights, so I had a bit of money in my purse from my pay the night before. I grabbed my purse, hopped on my 50cc scooter and went straight to the local shops, where I bought a second-hand Singer sewing machine from the sewing shop for $15. I balanced it between my feet in the foot-well of the scooter and tootled happily home. I was back within the half-hour and eagerly finishing my dress. My mother took one look and disappeared into her bedroom for the day, firmly shutting the door.

• • •

But back to killing my mother.

I had completed sewing the darts and side seams on my dress and was just trying to work out how to do the fluttery ruched end bit on the sleeves when my phone rang. The caller's name on the screen of my phone said 'Jane Mander'. Jane Mander was a frequent caller and was one of the few people who had access to my phone 24/7, even when it was turned to silent at night. Jane Mander was a long-dead novelist and journalist whose name was being used by the retirement village in Whangārei that my mother lived in. Other villages in the group are called Possum Bourne and Edmund Hillary.

I wasn't concerned about the call from Jane Mander, as the nursing staff who cared for Mum often called to let me know of changes to her medication or other practicalities that come with caring for an 86-year-old diabetic woman who can't talk or feed herself, and is paralysed, incontinent and suffering from late-stage Alzheimer's, post-stroke. I answered the phone with pearl pins in my mouth, ready to hear that Mum needed more or less insulin or more or less pain relief. Instead, the voice on the end of the phone told me that she thought Mum had pneumonia. She had woken with it and was not looking good.

I was surprised, as Paul had visited her the day before on his way to Auckland in the morning, and Dad had visited her in the afternoon. Neither had reported any noticeable change in her, although Paul thought she had managed to mumble the words 'you're gorgeous' to him, which was nice.

I was being asked by the carer on the other end of the phone if I wanted to proceed with the family's wishes not to administer antibiotics, and therefore not give her a chance at fighting off the pneumonia. I said 'Yes, do not give her antibiotics' before she'd even finished saying 'antibiotics'. This is what we had been waiting three long months for. The chance, finally, for Mum to end her suffering and humiliation at the hands of antiquated end-of-life laws which meant that she had to stay alive in her appalling condition. The carer then put me onto another carer to whom I had to repeat my request not to give antibiotics. And so I did. I was probably being recorded for legal reasons.

I asked the carer what would happen next and she was typically vague. One thing I have learned from dealing with carers of the elderly is that they never make clear statements about the welfare of the people they are caring for. I understood why, as family members can be a pain; if she had said 'come quick, she is dying' and Mum had stayed alive for another month or survived her pneumonia, she could possibly have got into trouble with her bosses and could have brought herself a large dose of full noise from a family that might be a bit distressed and difficult. The nurse simply said that my mother was comfortable, they had administered morphine and the next shift would call to update me when they took over at 3 p.m.

I put down the phone, spat the pins out of my mouth and went over to Dad's cottage, which is a short walk through our garage. Dad's cottage has the best view on our property. He makes the most of it by sitting in the La-Z-Boy chair that is plonked right in the middle of the lounge in front of the French doors, which provide him with expansive views of the Hokianga Harbour in all weathers. He gets so involved in that view that often the book he is supposed to be reading is left untouched for hours.

It hadn't occurred to me to get Dad's permission before declining antibiotics. He was the holder of Mum's enduring power of attorney and strictly speaking this was his decision to make, but early on in our dealings with Mum's care he had handed all responsibility over to me as he was exhausted, both emotionally and physically, and found himself unable to do it. The appropriate documents had been signed at Jane Mander and I was the go-to person for all things involving Mum. A decade ago Mum had written a living will because she didn't want to be left 'living like a vegetable'. Dad and I had made the decision together to put it in writing that no antibiotics were to be given to her, knowing that this is what she would have wanted.

I walked in and told him about the phone call. When I talk to Dad I always sit on the small couch along the wall, and often I'll put my feet up to join his on the foot-rest that extends from his La-Z-Boy chair. So that's how we had the chat about Mum dying. Him in his La-Z-Boy and me leaning back on the couch with both our sets of feet communing on the footrest.

Neither of us was particularly emotional because we were so relieved that the day had finally come. We had sat together in Dad's cottage and absorbed dramatic information about Mum on at least a dozen occasions during the past three and a half months. We had struggled to find answers on all of those occasions. What do we do? How do we do it? How will it affect her? Is this the best decision for her? But this time there was an answer. Mum would probably die. We also felt that this could take a while. You hear all the time of elderly people slowly dying, and indeed I had seen it happen around Mum in her care home. Walking to her room, I had seen several cadaver-like people lying unconscious for days in their beds, surrounded by family holding their hand and whispering kind things to them. I'll be honest — I would look at those families and think, when will it be my mother? Hurry up. Die.

'Do you think we should go over and sit with her?' I asked Dad. It would mean a drive of about two hours.

'Let's wait and see what they say at three o'clock,' he said. 'If she's on morphine she probably won't even know we're there.'

This reaction is very typical of my father. He's not emotional, not prone to over-reaction, and is grounded, sensible and practical in all things.

We didn't have to wait that long. As I tied off the last thread on my new dress and switched on the iron to give it a press, Jane Mander called again.

'I have just checked on your mother and I think you should

come soon. She is unresponsive and showing signs that she might not last long,' said the voice on the other end.

Wow, finally some definitive information.

'When you say "not last long", how long is that?' I asked.

'I can't say, but it is best you come.'

I made the decision that Dad should go and see her on his own. I'm not sure why. I still felt that it would take a few days, and to be honest I wanted him to be with her alone when she died. They had been married for 65 years and I strongly felt that this was their moment. Dad packed a few things he might need if he ended up being there overnight into the car and left straight away. I would follow later in the day to relieve him for the night if he felt the need to come home and rest.

An hour later Jane Mander called again.

'I am so sorry to tell you that your mother has passed away.'

Dad was still driving, only halfway there. He didn't have his cell phone switched on as he doesn't like to get distracted while he is driving. What to do? Should I hop in the car and speed to get to him and break the news? Was that even possible?

In the end I rang Jane Mander back and asked if they could intercept Dad at the nurses' station and sit him down and break the news to him. I would be there in due course. Then I sat down in my sun-room and rang everyone who needed to know. My husband, my children and my brother, Mark.

While I was talking to my son Daniel, he asked where his grandfather was.

'He's probably about to arrive at the care home and find out the news,' I said.

'Don't you think you should be in the car then and be there as soon as you can instead of talking on the phone? He's very old and he might faint or something.'

Daniel was right; what was I thinking?

Dad arrived at Jane Mander thinking Mum was just going to be in bed and not very well. Somehow he managed to get past the nurses' station and straight into Mum's room, where he gave her a kiss on the head. She was still warm, but after five minutes he sensed something wasn't right so went to find a nurse. She told him Mum was dead and he went weak at the knees and nearly collapsed. Sweet tea and biscuits were hurriedly arranged, and then Dad sat with his wife as her body slowly cooled off.

. . .

By the time I arrived, Dad was sitting with Mum's body and looking very uncomfortable.

People deal with death in very different ways, and my family is one of those that don't get 'carried away' with it all, as my mum would have said. My parents are atheists and raised me with no religion whatsoever. I have never read the Bible, and I have no idea about any of the Bible stories except what I gleaned from watching *Jesus Christ Superstar*. We do not believe in an afterlife.

Once you're dead, you're gone — no spirits or anything hanging around. You're just a shell. Dad wasn't keen on spending any more time alone with his wife's shell.

Dad and I hugged and had a bit of a cry together, and then I took a long look at my mother's face and body. The frustration and anxiety that had dogged her face for the past few months as she tried to work out what the fuck was going on had left. She was very pale and, well . . . stiff. I sat down next to her, because that is what you do, isn't it?

Dad got up from his chair after five minutes and said, 'Well, I'll be off then.'

I shouldn't have been surprised, knowing my dad's beliefs, but I was. For some reason I thought we should sit with her through the night as Māori do so that she was not alone.

'Are you sure you don't want to stay just a bit longer?' I suggested.

'I've been here for an hour, I just want to get home.'

It was about 6 p.m. on a cold, dark July night. It was raining and windy outside, and I wasn't sure this 86-year-old man who had just had a big shock should be driving anywhere.

'Just give me half an hour to sort things out here, then we can drive home together and pick up your car tomorrow.'

'No,' he said as emphatically as my dad ever gets. 'I'm driving home now.'

And so I let him go into the cold, dark night. He's a good driver and really I knew he'd get home okay.

I sat with Mum, and I'm glad I did. I think there's something in your brain that needs to be triggered by the sight of a body not breathing. I kept expecting her to fix me with those dark brown, expressive eyes of hers, which could cut me down in a millisecond if she was angry with me. But she didn't open her eyelids. I had a little cry, then carried on sitting there, still not wanting to leave her on her own.

I rang Paul, who was still in Auckland waiting to hear whether he should drive up that night or wait until tomorrow. I had no idea what to do.

'Should I stay the night Māori-style? Can I leave her? Is that okay?'

'What do you feel like doing?' said Paul carefully.

'Well I'm not Māori, so maybe not. Actually, I just want to get home and look after Dad. He's pretty freaked out.'

'Well do that then. But maybe call the funeral director first. Should I drive up now? Do you need me there?'

Paul is the son of funeral directors. He knows about that stuff, even though we weren't having a funeral. Mum's definition of not getting 'carried away' at the death of someone included not having a funeral where 'people tell lies about you'. It would be a simple cremation and a memorial at a much later date.

I told Paul to stay in Auckland for now. I was in crisis mode and I'm very good in that arena. I left Mum so that I could call the funeral director in the foyer of the care home — I didn't think it was appropriate for Mum's shell to listen to that conversation.

I sat in one of their luxurious armchairs in their beautiful hotel-like foyer and made the call, watched by the receptionist, who gave me a caring smile, and looking out at the rain reflected in the street lights.

I couldn't get hold of a funeral director.

Normally that wouldn't be a problem. Just leave a message and they'll call back. But in my crisis mode, I NEEDED ONE NOW! So for some reason I rang my brother-in-law Neil, who is a funeral director in Auckland, and made it his problem by crying down the phone. What he was supposed to do I have no idea — maybe push the special button all funeral directors have in their homes which says: 'Quick, Wendyl Nissen needs you!'

He must have made a few calls to Whangārei, as within half an hour I had a funeral director on the line and was arranging to meet her the next morning.

I returned to Mum's room and sat down again. I imagined Dad driving himself carefully home in the rain, and decided to leave. I tucked Mum in, for some reason, and when I left the room I left the lights on. Not that she needed them; it just felt right. As I closed the door I noticed that the nurses had placed a single orchid on her door. Obviously a universal signal for the carers that there was a dead body inside the room, but also a very touching one for me.

The drive home was long and wet and slippery, and not helped by the fact that my rear-vision mirror fell off halfway there. I got home and found Dad nursing a glass of wine in his La-Z-Boy.

I poured myself a glass and sat on the couch, heaving my feet up onto our shared foot-rest. We were both in shock, so we didn't say much except to express how relieved we were. I was glad it was just the two of us who had dealt with it. Dad and I don't need to exchange a lot of words to understand each other. If others had been there, it would just have added noise to what was a very peaceful and thoughtful half-hour on that Saturday night.

• • •

The next day, Dad stayed home and Paul met me at Jane Mander. We arranged with the funeral director to have Mum collected and cremated and we packed up all her stuff. It was nice just fussing around in her room and packing things into bags while she lay there. The sun was shining through her window and outside there were cows happily munching on grass. It seemed like a good thing that the time had come.

One of the nurses popped in to tell me how it ended for Mum. He could have said anything and I would have believed him. But I was happy to hear that she was basically unconscious the whole time on the morphine and died quietly.

I did feel that there should have been more of a fuss made by me. I should probably have been wailing and weeping, inconsolable, by my mother's bedside. And my father should have been there performing with me. And my brother. But it was just me and Paul, the way she would have wanted it.

The funeral director arrived with her trolley and set about transferring Mum onto it. As I watched, I felt very little. Then she put a shroud over Mum's body, covering her head, and looked at me. Waiting for me to do something emotional, I guess. I reached out for Paul, felt a bit nauseous and started crying on cue. It was, after all, the last time I would see my mother.

It was the weekend at the care home so there wasn't a full staff on duty, which was a blessing really. I had seen them line the corridors and stand silently with their heads bowed to farewell their residents as they were wheeled silently away to the hearse. I was very glad that didn't happen. I'm not sure why; I guess I just wanted it to be a simple process, free of emotion.

And that was it. A very quick, pragmatic death, finally.

CHAPTER 2

Normal but nice

When you grow up in a home that is not normal, you don't realise it is different until you spend a decent chunk of time in one that *is* normal. Then you start to think, 'Well, what is normal anyway?'

In the '60s and '70s, when I was a child, it was certainly normal for your mother not to work and to stay home as a housewife. Mine didn't do that and was the only mum of anyone I knew who worked. When I started school in 1967, my mother headed off to the teachers' training college because, in her own words, 'my brain needs exercising!'

There she became enlightened about feminism and hung out with groovy chicks who dabbled in the theatre and arts, didn't wear bras, sometimes smoked marijuana, ate Camembert and had fondue parties. She had discovered a world that was a long way from the suburban environment we lived in, where mothers baked and cooked sensible food, coddled their children and kept house.

In that era there was a tremendous amount of pressure on women to keep a tidy home, cook amazing meals and look absolutely gorgeous at all times of the day, with immaculate hairstyles, manicures and a great figure. The ideal home was one of domestic peace and tidiness. I know this because I saw it in my friends' homes. I think my mother struggled with these norms all her life and tried very hard to make our lives appear normal, even when sometimes they were anything but.

• • •

At just five years old, I would wake up in the morning and prepare to get myself ready for school. I had been well trained by my mother to get my breakfast, pack my lunch, get dressed and put my hair in pigtails, then get in Dad's car to be dropped off at school. Dad would let me hop in the car and start it to warm it up. I loved that. It was when Mum went to teachers' training college that I started getting myself ready each day. After that she was teaching, and so it continued. I thought this was normal. I remember once thinking that my friend Samantha had really lovely plaits and wondered how she did those herself, but that was about it. Samantha also had great lunches. Most days I bought my lunch because I had worked out it was easier to ask Dad for lunch money in the car than make my own.

Every evening my mother could be found in the kitchen doing battle. She hated cooking and resented having to do it after a day at work, but she had to. In the '70s the world was full of mothers dutifully cooking meals to feed their families. Mum mostly cooked chops dry in the oven, or sausages, also cooked dry. Or sometimes she would forget to take any meat out of the freezer before work so she would bash away at a slab of frozen mince in a pot on the stove until it succumbed and allowed itself to be cooked for a minute before a can of baked beans was added. Chilli con carne. We would eat dinner watching TV, then Mum would fall asleep on the couch. Usually by 7 p.m. I spent my childhood watching television at one end of the couch while my mother slept at the other. She always said she was so tired from working so hard. I believed her. Now I think it might have had more to do with the sherry she drank during meal preparation. This was normal.

Very occasionally we would wake up and find that the dining table was set with plates, cutlery and serviettes, and Mum was in the kitchen wearing an apron. She was cooking bacon and eggs, and we were told to sit down, in a light airy-fairy voice. She would serve us breakfast, complete with toast in a rack, a butter dish and a pot of tea with milk in a jug. While we ate, Mum would retire to the kitchen to pack our lunches, which would be unusually abundant with fresh bread and egg filling, a couple of biscuits and some fresh fruit. She would then brush my hair and plait it, then kiss me goodbye. This was not at all normal. It felt weird and odd; I didn't want to sit at a table and pretend we were a typical Kiwi family whose mother fussed over us. Like the rest of the family, I sat through it feeling like an alien. The next morning, I would make my way slowly to the kitchen wondering whether the 'happy family breakfast scene' would play out again today. Usually it lasted two mornings before we were back to looking after ourselves. This was normal.

Sometimes I would wake up and find that all our lounge furniture had been shifted around in the night. The couch was now under the window and the armchairs were now over the other side of the room facing the wall. This was normal, and happened every few months. The only thing that didn't get moved during my mother's nocturnal interior design activities was the piano. Too heavy. I used to think that other people's lounges were so boring for not having their furniture swapped around on a regular basis.

Sometimes my mother would chase my brother down the stairs with a beautiful orange enamel soup ladle, screaming her head off. It was very big and she'd bought it at an art exhibition because it had cool purple swirls on it. It made quite a good weapon with which to hit him. She never caught him, but she tried quite a lot. This was normal.

I liked to answer back to my mother when I became a teenager. I was fearless, and took every opportunity I could to flick her a one-liner as I left the room. This meant that I ended up on my knees with my brother holding my head in the toilet while my mother flushed it. My brother and I never got on well, and despite him having his own issues with our mother, he always seemed happy to lend a hand when needed. This was when he wasn't chasing me around the house and thumping the shit out of me. This was normal.

My parents had lots of parties. Most weekends. Waking up the morning after the party meant a wander through abandoned bottles and glasses, full-to-the-brim ashtrays and plates with bits of food, just to get to the television. The smell in the house was one of red wine mixed with smoke. One morning, all the crystal glasses had cracked in a fine line about two centimetres from their tops. Dad had played the trumpet so loud and high that the crystal had split. Well, that's what he told me. One morning a large table that lived in the hallway had been painted by the party guests. On it they had drawn a picture of a foetus. There was lots of red paint used to represent blood. I was about five. This was normal.

My mother loved to shop for clothes, and liked to buy them for me. Once I was trying on a dress. It was cream wool, a sort of '70s shirt-dress for winter. I walked out of the changing room, tall and skinny. She told me to turn around and then said: 'Oh dear, your bum has dropped.' I looked at my size 10 bottom and wondered what the hell she meant. She bought me the dress, even though it highlighted my defective dropped bum. This was normal.

My mother always took an intense interest in my boyfriends, who were all good-looking. She never liked any of them. But before she would declare her predictable verdict, they would have to be put through the 'meeting my parents' play. This would involve me introducing the boy to my parents, and then Mum would settle down on the couch and begin to recite a poem from memory. It was a poem I had written, which had been published in a special collection by my English teacher Miss Hall (who loved me) in my fourth-form year. Mum was reciting it to make fun of me. She loved that poem for how much she could make me squirm. I would blush bright red and beg her to stop, then wait for her to make a joke about it.

Not one boyfriend laughed. My last boyfriend, now my husband Paul, looked her in the eye and asked, 'Why would you do that to your daughter?' She quite liked Paul. The feeling wasn't mutual. This was normal.

• • •

There was a drawer in my mother's dressing table that was filled to the brim with pharmaceuticals. Mostly Valium, sleeping pills and painkillers. If I had trouble sleeping as a child, Mum would give me half a Valium. There was always a pill for what ailed me because that's what pills were for. To make the pain go away. This was normal.

Reading carefully through my mother's medical records after her death, I realised that she had struggled all her life with feelings of anxiety, panic attacks, depression and fatigue. Not one entry detailed her GP ever suggesting counselling or any help with these issues, which most likely arose from some sort of mental health issue. Instead, Mum would be given yet another prescription for Valium — 60 pills at once, every two months. That's a lot of Valium.

I'm sure she was not the only woman who had issues from her childhood that left her unable to function on a level she was expected to function at. I'm sure she had stuff going on in her head which at times made her act out in a way that was unusual, possibly frightening to her and harmful to her children. I know that sometimes it all got too much for Mum and she would disappear for a while. But that is the story around so many women's health issues at that time. Yes, we had the pill. Yes, we had feminism. But you still went to your doctor and were told you were just having a bad day or given some pills to help you feel better and perk up for the sake of a calm and happy family, home and husband. No one would have been remotely interested in helping Mum sort out the shit that was going on in her head.

Our home became a conduit for those head issues.

• • •

On the face of it, I had a 'good childhood'. I knew this because my mother always told me that, using her wonderful capacity for smoke and mirrors. My father ran his own PR business — one of the first in New Zealand — and had lucrative clients like Pye (who made stereos and colour televisions) and the adhesive company 3M. Mum, of course, worked as a teacher — although not for long. She found it hard-going, and eventually just worked as a relief teacher. I remember hearing Dad ring up her school principal on a number of occasions saying that Mum had to resign. She had to resign because she was having trouble coping emotionally, not that he told the principal that.

Money was good. We lived in a nice house in Birkenhead on Auckland's North Shore, and my brother and I had everything we wanted. I had ballet and piano lessons, and we always had holidays at a bach somewhere. My dad drove nice cars, as did Mum who had a sports car for a while. And we always had a boat. Because both my parents had come from deprived backgrounds, it was important for them to give their children what they hadn't been able to have.

For my mother, it was also very important that we put on a good show of being a happy, privileged family. Anyone who visited us found an abundance of good conversation, mainly with my mother, plenty of hospitality and sometimes some quite interesting art on the walls (sometimes borrowed from the library). But throughout it all my mother ebbed and flowed — took off at great speed, then crashed spectacularly. Wafted into a room in her new kaftan to greet visitors with a smile and a pottery goblet of wine, and then didn't get out of bed for two days.

I now think she worked very hard to deal with some sort of mental illness, which may have been bipolar or borderline personality disorder or just a tough childhood which left its mark and some terrible demons that she struggled to contain. Certainly she was prone to bad moods and sulking, meaning for much of the time it was like walking on eggshells — which for a child can be quite stressful. I never knew from one day to the next what mood my mother would be in, and so there was never a solid foundation of who my mother was to rely on. Would she be loving and caring and cuddly, or would she be dismissive, critical and plain nasty?

Shaming was a big part of her parenting tool box: ridiculing, belittling, putting down, keeping you in your place. I now know that this came from what happened to her as a child.

CHAPTER 3

Lost baby

FOR ADOPTION
Baby Girl, 4 months, for Adoption — Inquire Star 156.

— *Auckland Star*, 27 November 1933

This was how my mother found her 'forever' home. She was advertised in the newspaper — something which was okay to do in the 1930s when baby boys and girls and even twelve-year-olds were offered up for adoption. A flick through the classifieds from that time paints a sad story of unwanted children whose parents had abandoned them, and it was often felt necessary to include the word 'respectable' just to make sure that people knew this poor baby wasn't trash.

How my mum was adopted was a story she knew some of

the details about, but not all. She knew her birth mother's story, but not her birth father's. My mother died having never met her father.

• • •

Mum's birth mother, Eileen Gallagher, had been put out to work at the age of fourteen as a 'land girl', as was common in the 1930s. Girls were not to have careers; instead they would be sent out to work, usually in a domestic position, to contribute money to their family until they could find a husband. In New Zealand, girls would be hired to work on farms, either to help the farmer's wife with domestic duties, or to help out with farm work like milking. Eileen was working as a housekeeper with a family in Taranaki when she became pregnant at the age of seventeen, probably on her birthday.

She was sent home to her family in disgrace, and told her parents that she had been raped by the father of the family. In a way that was unprecedented for the times, the family believed her story. In the 1930s, if a girl got pregnant it was usually seen as her fault. She was a slut, a whore, a temptress, who seduced the man away from his wife and family for dirty sex. Teenage pregnancies were common, as the only contraception at the time was either a condom, which required the man to take some responsibility, or a back-street abortion.

Due to the strict morals of the time, these teenage pregnancies needed to be hidden. Often the girl was sent away to family elsewhere to have the baby, which was then adopted out. Or she was sent to a home for unmarried mothers and the baby was again adopted out. Sometimes the grandmother became the 'mother' of the baby in the family, and it was raised as a little brother or sister to the teenage mother.

Eileen's family believed that their daughter had been raped by the farmer and subsequently sued the father, who had children of his own, for paternity and support.

'It was even reported in the papers,' Mum said.

If it was, I couldn't find either the court report or the story in the local papers, despite a trip to Wellington where I spent two days poring over court records and microfilm of newspapers for the relevant years. It was at the end of the first Covid-19 lockdown and we were in Level 2, so while I was allowed into the Archives New Zealand building in Wellington, I wasn't allowed any help from the man at the desk.

Unable to interpret the massive books I was flicking through, I made the big mistake of asking him for some advice. This was after he had sat me in a chair two safe metres away from him and taken me word by word through the 'Welcome to the Archives' booklet I had already read. I realised halfway through the ten-minute performance that it was his chance to air the plethora of Dad jokes he had been working on during lockdown. Sadly, no advice would be forthcoming.

I assumed that a man with time on his hands might be willing to spare me some advice. But to do so would mean breaching the two-metre safe space between us for him to look at the old book I was pointing to.

'I'm really just here to make sure no one steals the furniture,' he said as he trotted back to the safety of his 'welcome desk'.

I retreated down the road to the relative safety and welcoming advice and smiles at the National Library, where one of the librarians had been corresponding with me online for weeks and had made sure that every edition they had of the *Taranaki Daily News* and the *Taranaki Herald* for the right time period were there for me to view. Thank god a librarian was able to safely show me how to work the microfilm machine without breaching the two-metre limit by getting me to watch her from two metres away. So helpful.

The reading room was limited to just ten people and there were only a few librarians at work in Level 2. At one stage one of them shouted, 'It's so quiet with only us here!' and was immediately hushed by her colleagues, in true librarian style.

I scrolled through microfilm after microfilm for two days, giving myself a massive migraine as a result. Unfortunately none of the relevant editions of the *Taranaki Daily News*, the morning newspaper in New Plymouth, were available and that was probably where any court case would have been faithfully reported.

I waded through articles nestled between news about New Zealand's first woman MP, Mrs McCombs, being sworn in, advertisements for cigarettes — 'My doctor has told me he smokes Craven "A" only, because of a delicate throat' — and the YWCA announcing 'an interesting and entertaining programme of nigger minstrel items'. Mr R.A. Candy's cow Violet, which he had bought for 58 pounds, in four years had produced 2489 pounds of fat; and there were dentists' advertisements for painless and free extractions of all your teeth and a perfect set of dentures for just two pounds. At the time I was nursing an infected tooth from a crown gone wrong in lockdown, and would have gladly paid someone two pounds ($126 in today's money) to have all my teeth painlessly extracted.

My attention was diverted by this example of paternity costs: 'Henry Charles Cunningham, who admitted paternity of an illegitimate child, was ordered to pay maintenance at the rate of 10s a week and confinement expenses (£3 6s).'

In 1933, the year of my mother's birth, ten shillings a week was equivalent to about $63 today, and the confinement expenses of three pounds and six shillings was equivalent to $459. Without a doubt, Eileen's parents had taken my mother's father to court for paternity and maintenance, which was quite common and quite lucrative in the early 1930s judging by the number of magistrates' court articles I read pertaining to payments.

There were quite sound reasons for Eileen's family wanting some cash, which I will get to later, and they were successful with their court case — although I didn't find this out for quite some time.

• • •

Eileen conceived my mother on or around her seventeenth birthday, and it was presumed that this was possibly not the first sexual encounter she had with the father — in which case she could have been as young as fourteen (her age when she started working for him) the first time, and that, legally, is a whole other matter.

Eileen was sent away to the Bethany home in Wellington for her 'confinement', where she kept herself busy embroidering nappies and shawls in readiness for her baby. She gave birth to my mother, whom she named Beverly, on 9 June 1933, three days short of nine months following her seventeenth birthday on 13 September 1932. As I later discovered, she was very much looking forward to bringing her new baby home, even though she was so young and unmarried. When she got home, however, her parents Edith and Harry had made no provisions for the new arrival. There was no bassinet or crib arranged, so Eileen emptied the bottom drawer of her dresser and turned it into a crib for Beverly.

Just a few days after settling back into the family home in New Plymouth, her mother Edith suggested that Eileen badly needed a haircut and sent her off into town to get one, assuring her that she would care for baby Beverly while she was gone. Eileen set off to town, where she rather enjoyed her appointment at the hairdresser's but was eager to return to her baby.

When she got home, Beverly wasn't there. Eileen never talked much about that day, even though it must have been her worst nightmare. She simply said that her mother had told her 'it was for the better'. She flew into a panic, searching every room of the house, shouting at her mother and sisters.

'Where is Beverly? What have you done with her?'

Only then was she told that Beverly had been advertised in the newspaper and had been delivered to her new home with all her belongings.

This is where you need to understand that Eileen's mum, Edith, who shared the same birthday as her illegitimate granddaughter and had no doubt spent her thirty-ninth birthday anxiously awaiting news of the birth of her first grandchild, was dealing with a few problems of her own. Her husband, the rather elaborately named Harry Alphonso Tregea Gallagher, who was the town clerk of Kaponga in south Taranaki, had been charged with theft of the Town Board's funds to the tune of 90 pounds ($11,000 in today's money) in February 1933. The court report I found says he got two years' probation, but others in the family believe he spent some time in prison.

Either way, money was short and the family was in dire straits as well as socially scorned after details of the court case were published in most New Zealand newspapers. A fresh start was proving difficult. This was probably the reason they decided to take Mum's father to court, which was a very public thing to do. It would naturally be reported in the papers, but possibly the

Gallaghers were already so publicly shamed that they thought they had nothing to lose.

• • •

Edith, born in 1894, was a twin, and one of fifteen children raised by George Joseph Harford and Elizabeth Annie Spurdle in Feilding. George Harford was a colourful character who had a drinking problem but found Christianity and sobriety through the Salvation Army. He later became a rather renowned Mayor of Feilding, who according to various newspaper reports was held in high esteem both during and after his mayoralty. One report refers to him as 'the father of the electrical power and lighting movement in Feilding', and another refers to a Chamber of Commerce motion that Johnston Park in Feilding should be renamed as Harford Park in recognition of his good work. The motion was not carried.

George was a keen bowler who toured Fiji with his bowling team after the death in 1923 of his wife Elizabeth, who was mentioned in dispatches as the 'widely known and highly esteemed' Mrs Harford following her death.

George was also the vice-president of the Protestant Political Association, which was founded in 1917 to counter the 'growing aggressiveness and assertion of the political aims of the Roman hierarchy'. This saw George touring the country to give rousing speeches, including one attacking James Liston, the assistant bishop of Auckland, who gave a St Patrick's Day address in which he described the Irish rebels involved in the Easter Rising of 1916 as having been murdered by foreign (meaning British) troops. The Rising was launched by Irish republicans to end British rule in Ireland and establish an independent Irish Republic while the United Kingdom was fighting in World War I. Many New Zealanders staunchly loyal to Britain took offence at Liston's comments, including my great-great-grandfather, who said in a speech on 22 March 1922 that 'Bishop Liston called suppressing rebellion murder, yet professed to love his country and be a loyal New Zealander. He should love the country well enough to get out of it.' When (during my research) I read this, I was quite impressed by George's succinct and cutting way with words. My mother inherited those genes and was very good at winning arguments.

Edith was a somewhat sombre and reclusive individual. Not much can be found about her early life, although she was a terrific piano player and organist. She taught children the piano and staged concerts with them, and played the organ in recitals and for the church, just as her granddaughter, my mother, did for her church in Fitzroy.

Edith married Harry in a hell of a hurry in 1915. I'm not sure whether she continued her musical career after her marriage to this young, handsome man from Bundaberg in Queensland, Australia. Harry Gallagher had all the right attributes. He was first and foremost a Salvation Army officer; he played trombone in the Sally band; he was a very fine baritone and a proficient book-keeper. His prospects and background were deemed appropriate for a union with the mayor's daughter.

Which was just as well, because when they married on 10 March 1915, Edith was three months pregnant with their first child — my grandmother, Eileen, who was born on 13 September later that year. Their wedding photo shows Edith in her Salvation Army uniform with a large white sash carefully draped over her stomach in an effort to hide her condition.

Harry was by all accounts a very clever man, but fond of the drink — in fact addicted, which meant that his association with the Salvation Army didn't last. One can imagine that Edith's life with Harry was always a little fraught. In 1942 she would eventually divorce the troublemaker after years of trying to hold the family together while he leapt from one elaborate scheme to another, legal or otherwise. Edith must have had some nursing or administration skills, because after her divorce she held the position of Matron at the Blind Institute in Auckland and at the Hikurangi Old Folks' Home in Whanganui.

Mum always described her grandfather Harry as being a bit of a rogue who looked like Einstein with mad white hair everywhere. She said he was a very intelligent man who was good with figures — but not quite good enough, it seemed.

• • •

When Eileen gave birth to little Beverly, Edith still had three other daughters to care for — Joan, Doreen (Dawn) and little Tregea (Gay), who was only eight years old — and the arrival of a baby granddaughter was probably more than she could bear, both financially and emotionally. Both of Edith's parents were dead and so she would have had no support from her extended family. It would seem that her only option was to have baby Beverly adopted out.

But having Beverly taken off her was not something Eileen was going to take lightly. Eileen had a strong character, an attribute she passed down to her daughter, who passed it down to me. She was well aware that because of Beverly, her family was now living on money obtained from the paternity case. How dare they now get rid of her?

As any mother of a newborn knows, those first few weeks are fraught with anxiety about keeping the baby alive. Was Eileen breastfeeding when Beverley was taken off her? Or had she been 'encouraged' to bottle-feed in preparation for the baby's removal? Many years later, I too would lose a baby early on — to cot death — and I know that feeling of suddenly not having a baby in your arms, not spending every hour of the day and most of the night caring for that dependent little thing that you made and had an intense bond with. There is a gaping hole where something once lived, and the despair and loneliness of suddenly losing a baby can be crippling. Eileen was only seventeen, and must have found it so hard to make that sudden adjustment from mother to girl again.

Eileen immediately set about questioning neighbours and her sisters about where her daughter was. She would not rest until she knew where Beverly had gone, because she fully intended to get her back. In the end, she twisted the name of the people who had taken her baby out of one of her sisters. Their names were Harold and Olive Peterson, and they lived in Fitzroy, New Plymouth.

'Right,' thought Eileen, 'I'll just ride over there and knock on every door in Fitzroy until I find her.'

Which is exactly what she did. Eileen took to going for secret cycle rides from her home in Eliot Street in the centre of New Plymouth out to Fitzroy, a ride of fifteen minutes, whenever she could. At the time Fitzroy was a small beachside suburb made up of several easily traversed streets criss-crossing their way down to the beach. It was more like a quaint English village than a suburb. Eileen cycled around, keeping her eyes peeled for a baby carriage containing Beverly or perhaps a baby in a front yard getting some sunshine. She allowed herself to imagine how Beverly would look. Would her dark hair have grown much? Would she still be the plump little baby she remembered her as? Would she be happy? Would she remember her?

On one of these rides, Eileen cycled down Clemow Road, thinking that she'd take a breather by the beach before heading home. As the bike made its way down the street, something across the road caught Eileen's eye. Washing was flapping on a line along the front porch of a small timber bungalow. She looked closer, and saw white cloth nappies. Before she knew it she had wheeled her bike across the road and peered over the front gate up at the washing. Nappies meant a baby.

And then she saw it. In the corner of each cloth nappy was a carefully embroidered name. Beverly. Eileen had painstakingly embroidered every B, E, V, E, R, L and Y in chain stitch, finishing off with a wee daisy, while she was pregnant and whiling away the days at Bethany in Wellington. She had found her daughter.

• • •

The seventeen-year-old who had given birth just a few months before could have taken a moment, hopped back on her bike and gone home for a bit of a think about how to proceed. But not Eileen. The urge to act in the moment and not wait another second was strong in my grandmother, as it is in me. Why waste time when you can stumble on in and get it done straight away? This approach usually has a 50/50 outcome. Sometimes it's a great success and you're so glad you plunged on in, and then sometimes it's a total disaster.

Eileen leaned her bike against the front fence, pulled down her summer frock so as to look a bit more respectable, smoothed down her hair, put her shoulders back and then marched right up to the front door and knocked.

Luckily for Eileen, the woman who answered the door was one of the kindest souls you could know, so her reckless actions did not result in a disaster. Olive May Peterson, Beverly's new mother, was a heavy smoker, a wicked card player and was on her second marriage after a rather tumultuous past. She had known hardship, sadness and grief at an early age. She knew what it was like to be lonely and alone and upset, as the seventeen-year-old girl standing on her doorstep was.

Eileen introduced herself, hastily explaining that she was Beverly's mother and she had a fairly good idea those were her nappies hanging on the line because she had bloody well embroidered them herself. She may have had her hands on her hips; I know I would have. Olive didn't hesitate to invite her into the home, sit her down and give her a cup of tea. I like to think they both lit up smokes as well.

Eileen was reunited with Beverly, now renamed Elsie Doreen (the Doreen came from Olive's older sister; years later, my mother would change her own name from Elsie to Elis). Olive encouraged Eileen to hold Elsie and play with her. I'm sure there were tears and a great deal of pleading on Eileen's part to get her baby back. But as she sat in the tiny kitchen at Clemow Road, part of her must have realised that here in Fitzroy her daughter had a stable, comfortable home, which was certainly not the case in the wake of her father Harry's crimes back at Eliot Street. She would also have sized up 32-year-old Olive and found her to be a kind, if a little worn, woman who already had four children and obviously knew what she was doing. For her part, Olive would have been looking at this poor young woman and doing her best to calm her down and make her feel comfortable. It's not every day your daughter's young mother turns up on your doorstep, but Olive was good at dealing with surprises, having had some experience of this in her past life.

Over the course of that visit, the two women came to an agreement. Eileen could visit any time she wanted, she could take Elsie for walks in the pram, whatever she wanted to do. She was welcome any time in the Peterson home and was encouraged to have a relationship with her baby daughter.

Olive walked Eileen out to the front gate and watched the girl ride away, turning to wave as she headed down the road.

• • •

Now that Eileen had found her baby, she needed to think about what to do with her life. She had domestic skills, so she could get a job. She had been taken advantage of and had had a baby. She had lost her baby. All by the age of seventeen. Things had to get better.

And so they did. Eileen got a job working in a jewellery shop in New Plymouth, and she also got herself a boyfriend.

The two of them would visit Clemow Road in the weekend and take baby Elsie for walks. Eileen enjoyed these rare moments of what was deemed normal life. For a few hours she could imagine herself as the mother of a young baby, just out for a walk with her husband before returning home for a nice cup of tea while her daughter had a nap, and then she would put the tea on and listen to the radio. Or something like that. Eileen was determined to be part of her daughter's life and it was all working out famously.

But then Eileen's boss saw her on her walk one Sunday afternoon, and said to her on the Monday morning that he had no idea she was married and had a baby. Eileen said she wasn't married, but she did have a baby. She probably had her hands on her hips this time as well.

That afternoon she was out of a job.

It makes me very proud of Eileen that she was not ashamed of her child. It would have been so much easier, and indeed advisable, to have lied to her boss and also her boyfriend, who must have known that the baby they were walking in the pram was hers. It was brave, and I love Eileen for that.

This event was a wake-up call for Eileen to get on with her life. She couldn't, realistically, spend the rest of her life mooning about Fitzroy in the weekends with a baby that wasn't really hers anymore. It was time to pick herself up and get on with her life. Elsie would always be there, but Eileen needed to break away and get a life of her own. Contact petered out for the rest of Elsie's childhood. There was the occasional card, sometimes a birthday present, but Eileen wasn't the best at keeping in touch regularly.

When Elsie was at high school, she went on a school trip to Whanganui for a basketball tournament between New Plymouth Girls' High School and Whanganui Girls' College. Mum knew that her birth mother now lived in Whanganui, and decided that she would visit her. Somehow she persuaded the family she was billeted with to drive her to meet Eileen. This meeting was kept secret for some reason. Even though Olive and Harold had always been kind and welcoming to Eileen, perhaps Mum thought it was best to keep things on the down-low for now. She would have hated to hurt Olive, who she loved so much. That visit prompted more contact, and a relationship between Eileen and her lost baby developed.

• • •

This is my mum's story of how her life began. She would tell it often because it was such a fascinating story, but it was also a way for her to say that she was wanted. When you consider that she was born into the fourth year of the Great Depression, to a young unwed mother whose family was in dire straits and publicly shamed because of the father's criminal offences, it could have been a lot worse. My mother was lucky to be adopted into a home that had Olive, who loved her, even if she was advertised in the newspaper. She could have ended up in an orphanage as so many illegitimate babies did in those times.

If only it had all ended happily there, with Mum growing up into a well-adjusted woman with a happy, fulfilled life. Mum did grow up. She had a life, but it was not always happy or fulfilled. Her childhood would leave her with severe trauma which would stay with her until the day she died. Because as much as Olive loved her and did her best to protect her, there would be a woman who came into that Fitzroy home who made Mum's life hell.

CHAPTER 4

Elis's two mothers

Elis inherited some characteristics from her birth mother. She was funny and as sharp as a tack, just like Eileen. But it was her adopted mother, Olive, who gave her empathy and understanding and a lifelong desire to help people.

• • •

When you're pregnant at seventeen, and your baby is taken off you, and then you find her again, your life has already been quite eventful. As happy as Eileen was to have found her daughter and to be allowed to have contact with her, things at home were not great. How could she forgive her parents for misleading her and basically stealing her baby off her? Whether Harry was in prison or not we're not sure, but if he was at home on probation and hitting the bottle, that can't have been pleasant. And if he was in prison, watching Edith try to feed all four of her daughters and handle the disgrace of her husband's downfall from town clerk to criminal can't have been pleasant either. Edith was, after all, the daughter of the great Mayor of Feilding, George Harford.

While Eileen was dealing with all of these things, she was no doubt noticing that friends of hers at the same age were enjoying a very different life. As I was trawling through those old Taranaki newspapers looking for details of my mother's paternity case, I couldn't help noticing the wonderful coverage of the debutantes who were written up and photographed in the society pages of the time. It was not hard to notice the photos of young women like Miss Joan Annette Tuck, the debutante daughter of Major Sir Reginald and Lady Tuck, whose engagement to Mr Hugh Davis had just been announced. Joan was wearing a lot of frills, a really big bow across her chest, and was holding a fan of feathers. Quite delicious.

Eileen was under no illusion that there would be a debutante ball for her, and knew that the best thing to do was simply get the hell out of Eliot Street. In the early 1930s, the only way to do that was to take a job as a live-in domestic, which was how she got into trouble in the first place, or work in a shop or find herself a husband.

So find a husband is what Eileen did.

Just two years after Elsie's birth in 1933, Eileen married Englishman John Swindells at the age of nineteen and promptly delivered her second child, Denis John Swindells, on 3 November of the same year. Maybe it was John's English accent that attracted Eileen, or maybe it was just a way out of hell at home with her mother and three sisters.

Not much is known about this marriage except that they moved to Whanganui and John may have been an insurance agent, but what we do know is that the marriage was not a success. The records show that when John Swindells enlisted for World War II in 1940, he was working as a barman in Auckland and Eileen was still in Whanganui.

Off to war John went; and Eileen was once again left on her own, this time with her young son, Denis. She applied for a benefit as a war wife, thinking it was the logical thing to do to survive, but she was in for a shock. The authorities told her that another claim had already been lodged on John Swindells — by his wife in the United Kingdom. John already had a wife in England and had been living in New Zealand as a bigamist. Poor Eileen. At just 25 she had lost a baby, had a young son and had now lost a husband.

Eileen divorced John on 18 February 1941, and before the war ended she had well and truly moved on. To another husband. During 1941, no doubt reeling from the knowledge that her former husband was a bigamist, she became friendly with the recently arrived Krsto Letica. Krsto and his two brothers had left Podgora on the Dalmatian coast of the then Yugoslavia in 1926. He and one brother, Nikola, settled in Whanganui while the older brother, Josip, went to live in Lyall Bay in Wellington. All three young men opened fish shops and restaurants.

Krsto and Eileen had a fish shop in Aramoho in Whanganui during World War II. Krsto told my uncle that he was forced to close the Aramoho shop after it was vandalised often by local 'rednecks' who assumed that any European must be either German or Italian and therefore 'the enemy'. Krsto never applied for New Zealand citizenship, so was deemed to be an alien during the war and was put to work in 'essential services'. He was part of a small team that built the huge boiler tower at the Whanganui Hospital.

Nine months after meeting Krsto, on 6 July 1942, Eileen gave birth to their daughter Kristi Tregea (named after her grandfather). To make things 'proper', Eileen married Krsto on 4 March the following year. This marriage was to last, although it was tumultuous according to my uncle Mike, who was born ten years after Kristi on 4 August 1952.

• • •

My mum was very close to Mike; he became her beloved little brother. She also knew Kristi, Denis and Krsto well.

At one stage in my life I mistakenly thought I was related to Krsto, possibly because I had heard so little of my true ancestry from my mother. In an interview for *North & South* magazine

I said that my mother was of Dalmatian heritage. She was horrified when she read it.

'We're not from Dalmatia! That was Eileen's husband, no relative of yours!'

I grew up knowing Nana Eileen, who visited once or twice when I was a child, from her home in Whanganui. Auckland was very much another country to her; we were her 'Auckland family', put on a slightly elevated platform, according to her son (and my uncle) Mike. I remember visits to Whanganui as a child, where Denis was always betting on the races and once pulled my hair in church when Mike was getting married to his wife Margaret. Denis was drunk and was hastily removed by someone. Kristi suffered from polio as a child so always walked with a limp; she was very attractive and full of personality. But it was Mike whom we knew well as a family and who loved Mum as his big sister. Her death hit him hard, I know, and her wish not to have any formal funeral arrangements made it hard for him to grieve for her.

Mike remembers Eileen and Krsto's marriage as difficult, with physical and verbal abuse being very common — most of it premeditated by Eileen. I can only imagine that Eileen was a bit grumpy, perhaps depressed and feeling that life had dealt her a very odd assortment of cards indeed. Money was always a problem and life was tough.

'My father's ability to have a verbal argument and stand his ground was reduced by his very limited English. His retreat was to disappear into his garden with his chooks until things quietened down,' says Mike. Most of the violence was over money (or the lack of it), and few arguments were resolved by talking.

Eileen had a job at Whanganui Hospital in the '60s, but during this time she applied for a position as Post Mistress at the suburban Gonville Junction Post Office. Despite having no formal secondary education or qualifications, she was appointed to the role. Uncle Mike says that she told her interviewer she used to assist her father in the office when he was the town clerk at Kaponga. This must have impressed the interviewer, because she got the job. She held this position until she retired.

Mike says he was a typical boy, playing every sport that was going, but Eileen had other ideas. He was enrolled in piano lessons and singing lessons, and was strongly encouraged along musical lines because, like his grandmother Edith, he was very musically talented. It seems that Eileen wanted something special for her son. Krsto died in 1964 when Mike was only twelve, so he was very much at the mercy of his mother's ambitions until he was old enough to resist and fight back.

'Eileen lost her ability to direct me in the way she wanted. Don't get me wrong — Eileen treated me very well, and would and did do anything and everything for me. She also absolutely adored every single one of her grandchildren and her own children.'

• • •

I once visited Eileen on my own when I was in Whanganui staying with a friend. I would have been about twenty and had begun to be fascinated by my mother's history, and I decided I wanted to get to know this woman.

I borrowed my friend's car and drove across town to see her. Eileen seemed quite surprised to see me. She was an outgoing woman, with a good sense of humour and quite cheeky, like my mother, but I don't have much more of an impression of her except that she was really nice and chatty. We had a cup of tea, and she gave me a red crystal necklace when I left. I still have it. She died a year later.

• • •

Olive May Peterson, née Prentice. What a dark horse Olive was. I have no idea whether my mother knew anything about Olive's past. If she did, she never mentioned it to me or my father, which made the day I discovered Olive's life history a complete surprise. A wonderful surprise, actually.

Olive was one of ten children who lived on Frankley Road in New Plymouth. Her father, William, was a gardener who had arrived in New Zealand from Worcestershire, England. He married her mother, Annie Wood, in 1896.

Everyone liked Olive. She was kind, generous and loving — but she also had a history. 'She was no angel,' my mother would say, with a glint in her eye. I always had the feeling that even though Olive had a bit of a past and was prone to tears and tantrums, Mum loved and admired her for it.

• • •

To me, Olive was a woman in round wire-framed glasses with short curly hair, peering at me from an old photo Mum had of her. You could tell she was kind because she had a nice smile. She died when I was a year old. All I knew of Olive was that she loved my mother unconditionally, and that she would chain-smoke roll-your-own cigarettes from the moment she woke up in the morning to the moment she fell asleep at night, lighting the new cigarette with the stub of the one she had just finished. Much of Mum's childhood was spent curled up in bed with Olive while she cuddled Mum with one arm, rolled a fag with the free hand of the other arm and then lit up.

After Mum's death I went searching for details of Olive's life, eager to find out who this woman was who had meant so much to my mother and who had saved her from being put in an orphanage. One chilly winter Sunday afternoon after a big day in the garden, I climbed into bed and got my laptop out. I had intended to have a nap while Paul read a book in front of the fire surrounded by cats and dogs. Instead, I logged into Ancestry.com and typed in Olive's name to see what came up.

There I found that Olive's maiden name was Prentice, and then I found that she had been married at the age of nineteen to a man called Percival Ronayne Coffey. Papers Past, where many of our old New Zealand newspapers have been digitised, then took over and sent me down a joyous tunnel of discovery until it got dark and Paul gently reminded me that it was dinner time.

Olive was pregnant when she married Percival (known as Percy), who was 45 on their wedding day, 2 March 1921. The premarital pregnancy was not an uncommon occurrence for those times, when contraception was neither approved of nor widely available. But the age difference between nineteen and 45 would have been a little unusual.

Seven months later, on 11 September 1921, their son William (probably named after her father, William) was born. Eighteen months after that Lenard was born, on 4 June 1923. I remember both these uncles from my childhood; I especially liked Len, who was a small man and very kind. His wife, Pearl, was particularly gorgeous to me and was a big reason I later named my own daughter Pearl. Mum said that Len had a hard time in World War II and it took him a long time to get over it. He rarely talked about it, as so many soldiers chose not to.

Olive now had a family, and a husband who was quite a star in the racing world. Percy Coffey appears often in the racing press as a well-known horse trainer in Taranaki, and later across the Tasman in the Sydney racing world. He was described in one newspaper article as being 'a fine trainer who would at all events prepare a horse for a dumping race. This was proved forcibly by the manner in which he turned out the New Zealand Grand National Hurdles winner of 1919, Compass.' In 1914 his horse Wild Lupin had been a surprise winner at the Kiwitea races, although one newspaper article suggests that it was no surprise to the 'Haweraites who raked in a lot of coin'. Percy was based in Hāwera at the time. The article went on to say 'This is not the first time that Percy Coffey has sprung a surprise on the public.'

Things looked good for Percy as his talents with horses began to shine, but his personal life was another matter. Back in his early twenties he had fathered an illegitimate child to Kate Adams. On 9 July 1901 he was ordered to pay seven shillings a week in maintenance to Kate, whose occupation was listed in electoral rolls as 'domestic duties' and her status as 'spinster'. In May 1905 he was before the courts for disobeying the maintenance order. The arrears amounted to ten pounds and three shillings. He had not paid any money since 9 October 1901, just three months after the maintenance order had been granted.

Percy did not appear, and was sentenced to one month's hard labour. You do have to wonder what good that did poor old Kate Adams in supporting her child. I'm sure Percy hated the hard labour, but she was still out of pocket and supporting a child on her own.

Reading between the lines, it would appear that Percy was in denial about his paternity of this child. Without DNA evidence it was up to the courts to decide who was the father of an illegitimate child, and in this case the courts decided it was Percy. He never really got with the programme: he was back in court in 1906, when he was fined ten shillings, and again in 1920 when he was fined twenty shillings. It certainly went on for a long time, possibly due to the determination of the mother. By the time Percy met Olive, that child would have been an adult and he would have been free of the financial demands of maintenance. It was possible that this time, with another illegitimate child on the way, he thought that, in his forties, it was time to get married and settle down.

Pregnant at the age of nineteen, Olive would have been relieved that Percy married her, even if he was 45 and not in great shape.

• • •

Percy was terrible with money, and appeared in court several times for non-payment of money he owed people. In 1919 he appeared in court because he owed George Gibson thirteen pounds, which is about $1200 in today's money. On 12 June 1924 he was before the court again, owing W.E. Jones thirteen pounds and twelve shillings ($1300), which if he didn't pay up would mean 22 days of imprisonment. This event is worth remembering because it had a terrible effect on Percy.

Percy was known as a man who was always 'hard up', which could possibly be because of his career as a race-horse trainer.

Perhaps he lived from win to win; maybe he gambled as well. Certainly his father, Martin Coffey, was bankrupted in 1880 in New Plymouth, so perhaps the inability to handle money ran in the family.

Sadly, by the time Olive came into Percy's life his glory days as a horse trainer were in decline. He was more hard up than usual, and by Christmas of 1923 things were looking bad for the couple. Their children, Bill and Len, were aged just two years and six months respectively when Percy decided to move out and live at the Normanby Hotel.

Normanby is halfway between Hāwera and Eltham in Taranaki, and this was where Percy had ended up basing his horse-training business. He could not afford the upkeep for his wife Olive and sons, so he moved out to the hotel. It is worth noting that a 'hotel' in Normanby in 1923 was far from luxurious. Percy would have had a small room without a bathroom, which would have been down the hall and shared by all the occupants. The rent for the room would have been cheap and would have included meals.

Olive spent her twenty-second birthday on 5 February 1924 at the home of local identity 32-year-old Tonga O'Carroll, who took the family in. Tonga was well known as an athlete and footballer, and held the Māori heavy and middleweight championships for wrestling. He was a fine young man, but he too had had some court issues. His family had sold 500 acres of what was called 'native land' in those days to the government for 12,045 pounds (just over a million dollars in today's money). The Crown had then sold it on to a new 'white tenant' for 13,810 pounds. The difference of 1765 pounds had been retained by the Crown, which they were not supposed to do. By law, Tonga and his family could not sell directly to a private person because they were 'natives', so they had no choice but to use the Crown as a go-between. Tonga took a petition to the Native Affairs Committee because the Crown had acted as a trustee for the 'natives' and in that role could not make a profit out of them. This case went on and on for years, and I could not find a conclusion. From the various court reports, however, it appeared that there was no willingness on behalf of the government to hand the money back.

Tonga was also the grandson of the very highly respected Dr P.J. O'Carroll, who worked closely with Te Whiti and the people of Parihaka after their health declined following the invasion by government troops and confiscation of their land in 1881. As I researched Dr O'Carroll's grandson Tonga, I became quite fascinated by him. Tonga was obviously a leader, a man you could rely on, and a bit of a hard case. At one stage he was accused of forging an invoice for two pounds, but the case was thrown out of court. For a while he was also a 'prohibited person', and was found drinking at the Okaiawa Hotel and fined. In my understanding, a 'prohibited person' in the early 1900s was someone deemed under the Licensing Act not suitable to be allowed to drink. There were a lot of these prohibited people before the courts at that time after having been found in hotels. It is probably useful to note that at that time all women were technically prohibited people as they were not allowed to drink in a pub or hotel unless accompanied by a man.

Tonga and his brother Harold also ended up in Hāwera Hospital in 1920 after a motorcycle accident near Ōhawe Beach.

So this is the man my grandmother Olive moved in with when things went pear-shaped with Percy. She lived with him for seven months, and while it may have all been quite above board with her simply being a lodger who probably cooked and cleaned for her family's keep, it must have been viewed by local society as shameful, simply because at that time Pākehā women did not associate with Māori men — let alone live with them!

Had Olive been abandoned by Percy when he moved into the hotel? During those seven months living with Tonga with two toddlers, what was Olive's life like? Certainly she would have felt deeply insecure about her future even if Tonga was providing her with a roof over her head. She was only 21 years old, with two dependent children and no income. That must have been frightening.

• • •

Olive kept in touch with Percy and often visited him with the kids at the Normanby Hotel. She and their little boys saw him on 10 June 1924, a Tuesday. It was in the evening and he had been drinking, but he wasn't drunk according to Olive.

Percy was worried about his court case in two days' time, when he would be expected to pay W.E. Jones the thirteen pounds and twelve shillings or go to prison for 22 days. He told Olive that he didn't know where the money would come from, and then said, 'A man would be better off in his grave.' Olive didn't take much notice of this because he had had a drink or two. When she said goodbye, he held his eldest boy, two-year-old Bill, and kissed him goodbye affectionately.

On parting, Olive said, 'Au revoir.'

Percy replied: 'No, not au revoir, but goodbye!'

By Thursday morning, Percy would be missing. He was last seen at the hotel on the Wednesday night at 10 p.m., but had not turned up to work in the morning. A jockey went to see the local constable to ask him to come and see the licensee of the hotel, who told him that Percy hadn't been in for his meals.

Percy had last been seen leaving the hotel in his work clothes on his horse Sly Wink. The constable managed to find Sly Wink, with saddle and bridle on, on the Normanby to Ōkaiawa road near the Electric Light Company power house on the Waingongoro River. A search was conducted all through Thursday until midnight, but they could not find Percy. The constable asked the Electric Light Company to drain the dam at their power house, and the search was continued at daylight on Friday morning. The dam was practically emptied, but no trace of Percy was found in the basin.

A group of Māori who had gone down the stream to catch

eels found him a short distance below the dam. Percy Coffey had drowned.

At the inquest held shortly afterwards, Olive gave evidence, explaining that she and the two children were 'stopping with Mr O'Carroll owing to Mr Coffey's financial difficulties'. She did note that on one other occasion, when a horse that Percy owned had died, Percy had also said he would be better off in his own grave. Tonga O'Carroll gave evidence that Percy had never said anything to him about taking his own life, although he was always 'hard up'. The constable giving evidence at the inquest noted that Percy Coffey was a sober and organised man.

Dr R.G.B. Sinclair, who examined the body at the morgue, found several wounds on the head that exposed the bone, but the skull was not fractured. He stated that the injuries were consistent with the suggestion that the deceased had met his death by diving from a height and striking rocks. The inquest finally found that Percy had drowned on 13 June 1924 'having left his ordinary haunts in a time of mental depression'. He was 49 years of age.

Tributes poured in for the well-known horse trainer, with his name being mentioned in numerous racing pages throughout the country, including the *Manawatu Standard*: 'The news of the death a few days ago of Mr Percy Coffey the well-known Taranaki trainer was received with regret in Palmerston North. In his young days Mr Coffey was a compositor but left that profession to follow the calling of a horse trainer. Among his many successes were Regulation, Compass, Darby Paul, To a

Tree, Lord Multifid, Wild Lupin, Khartoum, Depredation, Ngatiranui, Sundial and Encore.'

At the annual rugby match between the jockeys of the North Island and the South Island, a collection of 44 pounds was taken up on the ground for Percy's widow. Once she had paid his court fines of thirteen pounds and twelve shillings, if indeed she had had to, this would have left Olive with thirty pounds and eight shillings (about $3000 in today's money). It was a pity that those jockeys couldn't have helped Percy out while he was alive, but in those days secrets were kept and shame was to be avoided. Percy preferred to take his own life rather than admit that he was in financial difficulties.

It's not known how Olive was coping at the time, but I'm sure the money helped. She had her parents William and Annie, who were living in Devon Street in New Plymouth, and I'm pretty sure she would have been very keen to get out of Normanby after all the fuss. She probably stayed with her parents for a while before meeting the very Christian, very proper — and rather boring compared with Percy, I would imagine — Harold George Peterson, a hardware salesman.

Had Olive managed to shed the social stigma of being married to a down-at-heel albeit well-known horse-trainer who had taken his own life? Perhaps. Either way, Harold was prepared to marry her and adopt her two sons, and so just twenty months after the death of her husband Percy, Olive Coffey became Olive Peterson on 8 February 1926. It was just three days after her twenty-fourth birthday and a couple of months before Harold's twenty-second birthday.

The couple settled into 80 Gilbert Street, New Plymouth with Bill, aged four, and Len, aged two, who were now to be called Peterson instead of Coffey. Soon two more sons would arrive, Des and Terrance.

• • •

I'm sure that Olive was glad to settle into a more ordered life where bills were paid and there was no need to 'stop' at another man's house. I'm also sure that her experience with Percy Coffey gave her a lifelong understanding of the underdogs in society, although she might also have enjoyed a bit of glamour at the race course as the wife of a trainer. I like to think that she had a great time while it lasted. But her experiences would mean that she would always have an understanding of young women stuck with a pregnancy and no support or understanding. Even if this kindness led to her bringing a young woman into her house who would ruin her marriage.

Olive's experience with Percy also helps us understand why she never left her second husband Harold even when things got tough. She never again wanted to be on the street with no financial support for her children. Staying the course was probably well worth any humiliation and pain she would suffer.

CHAPTER 5

The biscuit jar

Mum's narrative about her childhood was relentlessly negative. She never had a good word to say about it, although occasionally things would slip out that hinted at reasonably normal childhood activities for the time — such as catching whitebait at the nearby river, picking blackberries for Olive to make into jam, playing many fun games of cards, playing the organ very well at church, knitting jumpers, or teasing her sister. There are photos of birthday parties, picnics and pets being cuddled. But there clearly was a darker side.

• • •

Olive Peterson was a kind-hearted person, which was why she had taken my mother into a home that already housed four hungry boys, four years into a worldwide depression. She liked to help people, which is something my mother inherited from her. Olive also liked to play cards, and liked to have 'dramas', as Mum called them. If her husband Harold upset her, which he often did, the tears and tantrums would be switched on full steam ahead. There would be sulks that lasted days — a skill my mother also inherited.

Harold mostly ignored Olive's dramas or went to church. He had an important leadership role at the Knox Presbyterian Church in Fitzroy, and wrote a history of it in 1976 for its 50th jubilee. He also spent a lot of time out the back of the house in his workshop. Harold was very good at woodwork and metalwork. Hanging on my lounge wall I have a piece of inlaid fret-work called 'The Maori Chief', which Harold completed on 1 December 1965. I know this because he has typed up all the details of the work, including which woods he used, where they came from and what machinery was used. Harold was like that. Organised. As a child, I also used a set of metal alphabet stencils he made for all his grandchildren.

Olive was never in very good health, possibly due to her chain-smoking, and sometimes spent time in hospital. It was there that she met an unwed mother who was about to have her baby. They got on well during Olive's stay, and before long baby Elsie had a sister. This woman, Mary, was invited to live with the Petersons as their housekeeper to help Olive, and she would bring her baby daughter with her so that she could also be adopted by the Petersons. It must have seemed like a great idea at the time — Olive wasn't well and had five children to raise, and Mary would be a lifesaver. Olive also wanted Elsie to grow up with a little sister to love. It was a kind thought — and Mum and her sister were indeed close all their lives, calling each other on the phone every day until Mum was no longer really able to when she got dementia in her mid-eighties.

By now the Petersons were living at 3 Princes Street, Fitzroy. Six children and three adults in a small two-bedroom cottage with a bedroom added on the back. We visited the house sometimes when I was a child. The kitchen was no bigger than a wardrobe attached to a small room which had an open fire, a small dining table, the electric oven and a radio. The internal toilet had been added on quite recently, but featured pieces of ripped-up newspaper attached to a string for toilet paper. This was the '70s, and I had never seen anything like it!

It was easy for me to imagine how my mother lived in this house because in the twenty years since she had left, nothing had changed — right down to the washhouse in the garden and the vege patch tended every day. There was also a lot of green. The house was painted green on the outside, on the inside, and everywhere else. It was the green that was popular back then; not lime, not sage, more of a Formica green.

My mother hated the colour green all her life.

• • •

Not long after Mary arrived into the home, she began an affair with Harold that lasted for years. The family knew about it (hard to hide in a two-bedroom home!), the neighbours knew about it — and the hypocrisy of a man who was a church elder and who insisted his family attend church every Sunday and follow the laws of the Bible hit Mum hard. One Sunday when she was a teenager, Olive and Harold had a fight that resulted in Olive lying on the bed in floods of tears, chain-smoking, and Harold taking off to church to do his important duties. Mum decided not to go to church to play the organ; an act of extreme rebellion in that household.

When Harold arrived home, red-faced with anger and outraged at her non-appearance — absolutely *ruining* the service for everyone — Mum stood her ground: 'I stayed to look after my mother, who you had been cruel to. What does the Bible say about that?' She got away with it. Score one for Mum.

My father describes Harold as a 'little Hitler'. He was a small man who ran his home with a rod of iron and very old-fashioned ideas based primarily on religion and male patriarchy. I remember him being somewhat removed into a world of his own where his every need was catered for by Mary. When I was a child, I only really had anything to do with him when he told me to sit on his knee and gave me a comb, then told me to comb his greasy, white Brylcreemed hair, which is quite creepy when you think about it.

The arrangement between Harold and Mary was embarrassing

for Mum, as it was discussed at length in the neighbours' houses and at school. Mum hated Harold for his hypocrisy, for being an upstanding member of the church yet carrying on an affair with his housekeeper in full sight of his wife at home. For treating her and her sister as girls were treated in those days: as second-class citizens. Mum did well at school, but was firmly told by her father that there were only two professions open to her under his roof. Shop assistant and typist. She took the typist option, but upped it to clerk and later legal secretary.

• • •

Mum wet her bed constantly through childhood and up until she was twenty. The reasons for bedwetting can be related to genes or delayed development, but Mum knew that the cause of her bedwetting was emotional stress caused by Mary, who hated her. Mum knows this because when she left home to fly to Australia — a trip she had saved hard for that was quite unique for the times and her social situation — the bedwetting stopped. Just like that. On her first night back at 3 Princes Street, it returned, and continued until she eventually moved out.

According to Mum, Mary's hatred of little Elsie came from her love for her own daughter. Primary evidence of this is the biscuit jar. Mary baked delicious biscuits for this jar, which was only ever to be opened by her daughter, who had exclusive access to it whenever she wanted. This is quite a pointed thing to do in a household with five other hungry children in the middle of an economic depression. From a very early age, Mum knew that she could never have one of those biscuits no matter how hungry she was, and her sister could have one whenever she wanted. It scarred Mum for life.

Mary also bathed, clothed and coddled her daughter in a way that Mum as a child never was.

In their teens, the two girls played basketball and, to Mum's delight, preferential treatment was for once out of Mary's reach. When Elsie was named in the top team for the year, Mary paid a visit to the coach's home and insisted that they had the wrong Peterson. It was her daughter who deserved the coveted position. Mum remained on the team, triumphant.

Olive had Mum's back, but increasingly, as she became more ill and lost her power in the home because of her husband's blatant home-based infidelity, her ability to protect Mum diminished. After Mum left school and started work as an accounts clerk she finally found some power of her own. She loved to save her money and buy clothes. Once she bought a very nice skirt; this caught the eye of Mary, who cornered her in the tiny kitchen one morning.

'Sell me that skirt. I want to give it to your sister.'

The answer was 'No.'

I was witness to this favouritism behaviour myself when my cousin, Mary's granddaughter, and I went to stay with Mary and

Harold for a week of the school holidays. We were both about eleven and were excited to be flying down to New Plymouth from Auckland; our first time on a plane.

We stayed in the room out the back, were taken to church, bowls and bingo, and visited relatives for endless cups of tea and cake. When we met these friends and relatives, Mary would clearly say, 'Isn't she beautiful!', pointing to her granddaughter and not mentioning me at all. I didn't mind. My cousin *was* beautiful, although I wasn't exactly ugly. Mary would also leave me at home with Harold while she took my cousin out on 'special adventures, just for us', returning with gifts she had bought her granddaughter.

Then Mary set us both up to make scones. She put the ingredients out on the table and encouraged us to make a batch each. I enjoyed this, as it wasn't something my mother did with me at home; she hated baking. Mary instructed us individually on what to put in the bowl and how to mix it and then cut up the scones. When they came out of the oven, my cousin's were perfectly risen and mine were flat rocks.

'You forgot to put the baking powder in,' said Mary, laughing at me along with Harold. 'What a silly girl not putting in the baking powder,' she repeated for extra emphasis.

I knew I hadn't forgotten, because I hadn't actually been told to put baking powder in. I had been set up. I didn't say anything, but already at age eleven I knew something was up.

Absolutely none of this really worried me, but I must have

said something to Mum because I never went back there for school holidays.

Olive would come and stay with Mum in Auckland, and used to call me Joy when I was a baby because she thought I was so perfect. She died when I was just one year old, and soon afterwards Harold and Mary married. They too would visit, driving up in Harold's immaculate car and always bringing frozen whitebait. I guess Mum's hatred of both people was well hidden if she allowed them to come and visit. I also remember being looked after by Harold and Mary when Mum and Dad went away. I remember it because I had a huge fight with Mary, who wanted me to wear a twin-set which was popular at the time because the Royal family wore them over pleated tartan skirts. I wanted to dress like a child of the '60s. I was only about seven but got a big telling-off at the time from Mary — and later my mother.

• • •

In Mum's childhood there was certainly emotional abuse and cruelty from Mary on a regular basis, along with the feeling from her that she wasn't really wanted or needed in the family unit. Olive was the one person who truly wanted and loved Mum, but her power was limited. She was also hardly a saint herself, as she'd often escape the madness of her home to play cards and possibly drink elsewhere for hours on end.

Harold's behaviour, Mary's abuse and Olive's inability to protect her all lined up to leave Mum pretty damaged. She had a lifelong and deep-seated fear of infidelity. If any woman so much as looked a little bit too long in my handsome dad's direction, she was cut from their social circle, immediately. Mum curated a long list of women she hated for mostly imagined crimes against fidelity; in one case, instead of getting an anaesthetic at the dentist, Mum would simply feel the pain and project it at this woman. For years. It would be fair to say that it ate her up.

When I was in my twenties and flatting, I got a call from Dad one night to ask whether my mother was at my house. She'd disappeared during a movie at Mission Bay. Mum and Dad had been having a night at the movies with Mum's sister and husband. As they were walking to the theatre behind the other couple, they noticed that Mum's sister's skirt had got tucked into her undies. Dad simply reached over and pulled it down, and she responded with an 'Oh, Cedric, you naughty boy' type joke.

Ten minutes into the movie, Mum left to go to the bathroom and never returned. They searched everywhere, and then Dad went home to wait it out. Sure enough, Mum turned up in a taxi after midnight. She accused Dad of hitting on her sister, which of course was ridiculous. But somewhere in Mum's head that action had triggered something catastrophic and she had had to run. Perhaps it was something from their childhood; we'll never know.

Mary's influence was disastrous in other ways. That biscuit

jar was to set up in my mother an obsession with food which never left her. She was overweight most of her life, was always on a diet, and hoarded food in cupboards and freezers, constantly afraid that it would run out. After Mum's death I found her diary from 2016, just a year before the dementia took hold and two years before she died. On 31 March is firmly written 'start the Zone diet!'

Being overweight led to diabetes in her forties and massive self-esteem problems. My mother hated her body, and everyone else's. If you went anywhere with Mum she would begin a constant stream, both in her head and out loud, about the body shapes she was witnessing. 'God, look at her bum, it's huge,' or 'Now *that's* a slim figure.' I dreaded her asking, as she did quite often, 'Quick — look at that woman over there, am I as fat as her?' There is no right answer to that question, so I learned very quickly to say, 'I'm not sure, she's a lot taller than you,' to distract her. Once when I was taking her shopping and pulling into a parking space, a woman was walking alongside. 'Skinny bitch!' snapped Mum, for no apparent reason except that the woman had the misfortune to be slim and in my mother's gaze.

'Here comes chubby,' my mother would say every time she saw one of my daughters. 'She looks like a sausage,' she would say of one of their friends. Girls were made for Mum to criticise their bodies. The closer they were to her, the harsher the criticism was. Eventually I told her to stop talking about my daughters that way.

My mother taught me to sum up a person by how they looked, not how they were as a person. When I realised this, I had to work really hard when I met a person for the first time to look into their eyes and listen to what they were saying rather than stand back and work out whether they had a 'great little figure', as Mum would say, or were 'awfully tubby'. I still sometimes catch myself doing it to this day, but manage to pull back and value the person I have just met for who they are, not what their physical shape represents.

Mary's constant put-downs of Mum left her with depression and anxiety, which stayed with her all her life. Reading through Mum's medical records, I was shocked to see how often she had sought help for these things, yet she had never talked to me or my family about them. She was on some pretty major pharmaceuticals to help her cope.

Finally, Mum had to be right. In all things. Having been told she was wrong and insignificant all her childhood, she emerged determined to know everything and be right on every fact. This could be very annoying.

• • •

To be fair to Mary, it's useful to look at her situation. An unmarried mother in the 1930s was not a good thing to be. She would have certainly had to put her daughter up for adoption if Olive hadn't taken them in. Once safely ensconced at Princes Street with Olive and Harold, she wanted the best for her only child and did everything in her power to achieve that.

Perhaps she and Harold were genuinely in love, perhaps she just used him to get power in the family, or perhaps he was a predator who forced her into the relationship; we'll never know, and it doesn't really matter. Mary did her best to raise one girl, and in the process damaged another. I'm also sure that in that era you wouldn't have had to look too far to find other men like Harold. He made the most of being a white man in a world where white men ruled the roost. His personality enjoyed being the boss and having not one but two women at his disposal in his home. Mum attended his funeral, but wild horses couldn't have dragged her to Mary's.

• • •

Looking at Mum's situation at birth with her grandmother Edith's stresses, she was lucky that she landed in a home where she was fed and clothed, kept warm and learned how to play (and cheat in) a mean game of cards. But as we learn more about the intricacies of child-rearing, we come to know that it doesn't take much to set up a whole lot of pain in a child during their formative years. And as we are learning, that child will often take that pain and pass it on. My mother certainly did that.

CHAPTER 6

The trouble with food

Scratch the surface of most women in the '70s and you'd find a mad dieter. It seemed to me that in the '70s everyone was on a diet of some kind, and my mother was on them all.

She went to Weight Watchers once or twice a year to have another go at losing weight and put herself through the fat-shaming that this organisation indulged in. Women would turn up, having faithfully followed their diet sheets, and get weighed in front of all the other women — and if you hadn't lost any weight you were given a little pig. As I'm writing this I can't quite believe that happened, but it is clear in my memory that the whole point of Weight Watchers was to get women together in a room, charge them a fee and then make them feel like shit. And I clearly remember Mum bringing home a little pig and shamefully putting it on top of the television one night. Perhaps it was just that her group was run by a particularly nasty sort of person, or perhaps it was more widespread; I have no idea.

I experienced Weight Watchers' fat-shaming myself in the '80s after the birth of my second child, when my mother suggested I sign up to the local group to lose a bit of my 'baby fat'. Honestly, I was a size 14 for god's sake. I lasted two weeks, during which time the leader of the group idolised and shone a favourable light on one woman who skipped up to the scales every week and had lost two kilograms, just like that! Every week. I was convinced it was a scam that the golden girl and the leader had set up to be 'encouraging'. But the golden girl Weight Watcher was not going to encourage or help me lose weight, so I left and the weight dropped off anyway, as it does after you've had a baby if you just let it.

• • •

Two of the main features of diets in the '70s were deprivation and product placement.

Mum would buy whatever was the latest fad for losing weight, and would hide these items in her bedroom so we couldn't eat them. Which was quite difficult during the Ayds phase. These were little chewy caramel appetite-suppressant sweets that women trying to lose weight would eat between meals. They tasted delicious and came laid out like little dominos in a flat box similar to a chocolate box. It must have been so hard for Mum to just eat one of these between meals and I doubt she did.

Then there were the delicious bright pink cans of TaB, which contained a Coke-like drink with artificial sweetener and only one calorie, a very early precursor to Diet Coke. We never had soft drinks in the house, so these were the ultimate in treats for us. But no, they were Mum's, and occasionally we could have a sip if we were really good.

Frozen yoghurt was another fad, along with anything with saccharine in it. Suddenly there was no sugar in the house, just saccharine, and my brother developed whopping great wart-like growths on his fingers from eating too much of the stuff. We had saccharine in coffee and tea, saccharine sprinkled on Weetbix, and a saccharine-laced cordial called Thriftee. When we stopped using it, the growths on my brother's fingers went away.

I've lost count of the many diets my mother went on. The Grapefruit Diet was where you ate half a grapefruit before every meal because apparently it contained an enzyme that burns fat. The Sexy Pineapple Diet had you eating pineapples two days a week for similar *faux* reasons. In the 7 Day Milk Diet you replaced every meal with a glass of milk because there were micronutrients in milk that minimised fat deposits.

And then there was the Israeli Army Diet, which was big with Mum for a while. It had absolutely nothing to do with the Israeli Army, but never mind. The promise was that you followed it for eight days and lost shitloads of weight. For the first two days you ate nothing but apples, the next two days nothing but cheese, the next two days nothing but chicken, and for the last two days nothing but salad. You were also allowed black tea and coffee. It seems totally crazy now to even consider eating like that, but thousands of women did, including my mother, myself and lots of our friends. The weight came off, but was back again very quickly.

By far my mother's favourite diet was the Atkins Diet. Oh how she loved the fry-ups of bacon and eggs and putting cream in her coffee around the clock. Loads of meat and not a carbohydrate in sight. It was the first of the low-carb diets to hit town and Mum bloody loved it. You knew if it was working because your breath smelled like nail-polish remover. This was a great thing because it meant that your body was in ketosis, which means it is burning fat for energy. Yay! Mum would breathe on me with delight.

'Can you smell the ketones? Can you? I'm burning fat!'

She would be so delighted that she was in a ketosis state, just willing those pounds to disappear.

• • •

Despite the '70s diet fervour, my mum never lost weight for long. I remember she lost quite a chunk when I was overseas on a student exchange for a year when I was seventeen. I wasn't around to see how she did it, but she seemed very happy with how it all turned out — until she put it all back on again, and some more for luck, within the year.

The next big weight loss came when I had my first child, Daniel, in 1986. Mum's doctor congratulated her on the birth of her first grandchild, but then told her in no uncertain terms that if she didn't lose weight and control her diabetes she would not live to see him turn ten. That really got to Mum and she managed to drop the pounds again. But again, not for long.

I've thought a lot about what it means to be not only obsessed with food, but also deeply worried that it would run out and to desperately need it to soothe and calm yourself. My mother used food as a reward, as a means of calming and settling herself, and sometimes just because she was bored. It didn't really matter which. Food made her feel good and she would eat it and eat it, sometimes to the point of vomiting. She also hoarded food; her kitchen cupboards were filled to the brim with cans and packets and jars of the stuff. At one stage she had three deep-freezers full of food, just in case.

All of this can easily be traced back to her childhood. The longing for a biscuit from the forbidden biscuit jar and the determination that when she grew up she would never, ever be deprived of food again. Mum always had a very strong drive to eat. If anyone ventured to suggest that she might have had enough chocolate biscuits for one sitting, as my father sometimes (bravely) did, she would snap back, 'I can eat what I like, when I like.'

And, of course, she could. She would never again be deprived of that biscuit jar of love.

Unfortunately, with her diagnosis of diabetes came the message that she must always carry a snack with her in case she suffered from low blood sugar, and should never go too long between meals. Well that, right there, was a passport to constant eating. My children grew up knowing that Grandma always had barley sugars in her bag should they want one. Not to mention the odd banana and chocolate biscuit.

Losing weight is something most women have tried to do in their lives. Not all of us are born 'skinny bitches', as Mum called them, and some of us go through stages in our lives when we put on weight, usually following pregnancy, because of illness, or just because we are unhappy and are eating our feelings. Unfortunately none of us is told that this is perfectly normal and to just ride it and not panic, and therefore not develop dangerous eating patterns involving deprivation then binge-eating, or bulimia or anorexia.

Some women, like my mother, develop illnesses like diabetes that really would benefit from them losing weight, but by then the damage is done. Their relationship with food is mangled and distorted and they don't know how to eat normally. I doubt that my mother ever knew what hunger really felt like because her stomach was never empty.

In recent years we are beginning to realise that food can heal. Eating the right foods can keep our stomach microbiome (population of beneficial bacteria) healthy and provide us with essential vitamins, minerals and fatty acids to allow our body to be nourished and to heal. Food is no longer the enemy; it is our friend and something we can use to help ourselves. For my mother, food was both enemy and lover. She hated it, but needed it to feel normal and loved. It was never her friend.

CHAPTER 7

The gentrification
of Elsie

When Elsie Peterson met Cedric Nissen she couldn't believe her luck. She and the girls she worked with at the accountants' office in town had seen him walking to and from work at the offices of the *Taranaki Daily News* in New Plymouth. They all thought he was a 'dish'.

Elsie arranged for one of the girls — who knew someone who knew Cedric — to invite him to a party that she and her sister were having while their parents were out of town. Cedric turned up at 3 Princes Street, Fitzroy, and was delighted to see that there was a box of beer under one of the beds. The fact that Mum had had a party in Fitzroy in 1952 with a bunch of teenagers and a box of beer under the bed surprised me. Surely that was a very daring thing to do in those days, especially in that household.

The two became a couple, but there was just one problem. Mum had worked hard and saved for a 'working holiday' in

Australia. She and her best friend had bought tickets on the flying boat to Sydney and planned to stay for six months over the summer. Flying boats were very new and very flash for a girl like Elsie from Fitzroy. The first flying-boat service from Sydney to Wellington launched in October 1950.

'Everyone said I should cancel the trip and snap up your father, but I didn't,' Mum told me proudly. While she was in Australia, she worked for Davis Cup Tennis in Adelaide and generally had a wonderful six months of working and fun. 'They all said he wouldn't be there when I came back, but he was.'

Cedric drove down to Wellington to meet Elsie off the flying boat at Evans Bay, and that was that. They would get married shortly afterwards, on 6 June 1954.

Elsie found work as a legal secretary in Wellington, and Cedric enrolled at Victoria University to do a veterinarian's degree. He had worked for a vet in Rotorua as a teen and was keen to see if he could become a vet. They found a flat on Oriental Parade, and set about having what will always be described as some of the best years of their lives.

In a decision that was very advanced for their era, they opted not to have children for five years. In the 1950s most women who got married settled straight into motherhood, but Mum wanted a few years of fun working and playing with her new husband first. This may have arisen from the knowledge that the lives of both her birth mother and her adoptive mother were badly affected by teenage pregnancy; or Mum might just have felt that life in Wellington with Dad was fun and she didn't want it to change. There were parties, and just enough money, and a shared flatting situation with her sister and a female cousin. There was a fair bit of tut-tutting from the neighbours, but they tolerated this liberal and racy '50s lifestyle of mixed flatting.

Cedric's veterinary degree did not eventuate, possibly because of the party-hard lifestyle he and Mum were leading, which didn't leave much time for study. When Elsie gave birth to my brother Mark on 28 August 1959, Dad finally decided to call vet training quits and go back to journalism. He got a job in Auckland on the *Straight Furrow* farming magazine in the Auckland Star building on Shortland Street, where years later I would begin my career.

• • •

During the five-year hiatus before succumbing to pregnancy, Elsie set about learning how not to be Elsie. She was not alone in a generation which, born in the disastrous 1930s, sought to make a better life for themselves and climb the social ladder. It became very important for my mother to be seen to be middle class, because she desperately wanted to leave her working-class Fitzroy childhood behind her.

She got on well with her lawyer boss in Wellington, who would often lend her his palatial home to stay in when he and his family went away. She studied him and his lifestyle closely and taught herself some manners. These included never, ever putting the bottle of milk on the table; you poured it into a milk jug. You kept your mouth closed when you were eating, and took small, lady-like bites of food. You knew which fork went where, which knife to use and where to place the serviette. You didn't start eating until the hostess had started. You never took seconds unless you were offered them, and you never left the table without asking first. And you never, ever licked your fingers.

These rules of etiquette will be familiar to many, but to our family they were the law. Shortly after I started going out with Paul, we had just finished some fish and chips and he started licking his fingers. I looked at him in absolute horror and shouted, 'Don't do that, it's *common*!' — quite unconsciously parroting my mother.

He laughed his head off and kept licking. My childhood had reared its ugly head. Paul said he wasn't about to stop licking his fingers just because my mother didn't like it. I begged him to at least not do it in front of her. He didn't, but even to this day I always get into a slight panic whenever he does it.

Next on the list for the gentrification of Elsie was to get rid of her awful name, because that was really common. Of Scottish origin, the name Elsie was a constant reminder of Mum's humble beginnings. Elise would have been better, but Elsie had to go.

Once my parents had moved to Auckland and had settled into an old villa on Northcote Point that they shared with Mum's sister and husband, Elsie decided to become Elis by deed poll. While she was at it, she changed my name as well. I had been named Wendy Mordue Nissen (Mordue being my nana's surname and my father's middle name) when I was born in Auckland on 19 July 1962, but after a year my parents decided the name wasn't right. Dad says it was his idea to put an 'l' on the end of my name just in case I became famous and needed a name that stood out.

So in 1963, Elsie became Elis and Wendy became Wendyl. We were both gentrified at the same time.

I hated the name Wendyl growing up, and insisted that everyone call me Wendy. Then when I started work at the *Auckland Star* and had a byline, I decided to use my proper name. However, if I'm booking an appointment I often just use the name Wendy because people don't know how to spell the name Wendyl.

Once I booked an appointment at a doctor's office, and said to the receptionist when she asked how to spell Wendyl, 'It's Wendy with an "L".' When the doctor came out to call me, she said 'Is Lendy here?'

Both my parents spoke 'very well', which seemed to be very important to Mum. Dad's mother was British, so he grew up speaking the Queen's English, and both he and his older brother Arthur did some broadcasting work at some point in their lives. Dad read the news on South Pacific Television at the weekends in the '70s, and Arthur worked for the local radio station in Rotorua in the '50s. Mum worked hard to speak well too, especially when answering the phone, but occasionally the Fitzroy drawl would slip back in when she was angry or drunk.

Living in Wellington and then Auckland exposed my mother to a society that she had never known in her small-town childhood, and she rose to the challenge. There were regular visits to the Mercury Theatre to see plays, and some of the actors became her friends. There were regular visits to the Auckland Town Hall for concerts, and one of Mum's favourite haunts was The Mill in Durham Lane, where she would buy pieces of pottery and art with which to adorn our home in a very cultured fashion.

I have to say that I appreciated those concerts and theatre visits: they helped shape my love of both. And Mum's pottery, which I have inherited, is really lovely and of very good quality, representing some of our top potters of the day.

It was also very important to keep secrets about Mum's previous life, in case she was 'found out'. I've heard both my mother and my aunt in conversation be very vague about their beginnings. Once when someone said they both looked so alike, which obviously they didn't because they were not blood relatives, they both smiled and nodded and agreed. Easier to do that than explain their adoptions and their unwed teenage mothers.

I became very used to watching the dance of vagueness that my mother would perform every time the conversation came around to her childhood. It served her well, because everyone thought Elis was top-notch, well bred and well educated. My mother was a master of smoke and mirrors.

CHAPTER 8

Dad, the quiet one

Anyone who knew my parents knew that Dad was the quiet one. Good-looking and quiet. Just how Mum liked it.

Dad did not have an ideal childhood — there were many things that he could have let scar him for life — but unlike Mum he seemed to emerge fairly unscathed, and has always been quite an amenable person with a pretty happy outlook on life. I think this was because his mum loved him unconditionally and constantly; there was none of the cruelty and emotional abuse that were features of my mother's childhood. Dad was the apple of his mother's eye, a dead-ringer for his father, and, despite being poor and fatherless from the age of seven, he emerged as a talented young teenager who shone as a competitive swimmer and First XV player, and entered the world as a young adult brim-full of hope and talent.

Dad spent much of his youth out on his friend John Lewis's

farm, which seemed to shape him for life as someone who loved animals and rural life. He and John would spend their days riding horses, helping drench the livestock, and generally hooning around John's farm enjoying teenage life outdoors. Dad never got to live that life, due to my mother's hatred of it and her love of the city, but he does now, living in the cottage attached to our house in the Hokianga.

• • •

Dad's mother, Marguerite Beatrice Mordue, known as Trixie, was English; his father, Arthur George Nissen, was a New Zealander with Danish immigrant parents. Their relationship had all the hallmarks of a wonderful wartime romance. They met in England when Arthur was a Warrant Officer class II and Command Sergeant Major in the 3rd New Zealand (Rifles) Brigade and she was one of the 7000 British women who served in the WAAF, the Women's Army Auxiliary Corps. They were both stationed at Brocton Military Camp near Stafford in the West Midlands of England.

While looking in a box of photos for a picture of my mother's birth mother Eileen, I found a little card just slightly bigger than a matchbox. As I pulled it out of the box, I slowly realised that this little piece of cardboard was a dance card covered in handwriting and it was more than 100 years old. It was the first evidence of a romance forming between my grandparents. My nana must have saved it as a memento and somehow it had survived throughout her life, as well as most of my dad's life, and had ended up in a box of old photos I have had lying around for 30 years. Thinking back, I think I found it when Mum and I were cleaning out Nana's cottage after she moved to a care home. I must have tucked it away thinking it was interesting, and then promptly forgot about it.

The dance card was for the WA(NZ)AC HAKA to be held on February 12th, 1919 in the 'N' lines Whare, Brocton Camp. Under the date it says 'THE DINKS AND THEIR PETS PARTICIPATE.' In Brocton Camp the New Zealand soldiers were nicknamed 'The Dinks' as they were considered to be good, honest (dinkum) soldiers, and I'm guessing their 'pets' were their girlfriends.

One of the three masters of ceremonies for the evening was my grandfather C.S.M. (Command Sergeant Major) A.G. Nissen. Opening up the card, I found that of the 16 dances listed, the initials A.N. were firmly written beside every second one. Arthur and Trixie had danced to a waltz called 'We've clicked', a maxina called 'Oh! I s-way' and a destiny waltz called 'Three minutes of heaven'.

I would imagine a dance like that must have brought so much joy to these young people. Arthur was only 23, yet had been at the Western Front, fought valiantly, been wounded and gassed, and had been promoted to Sergeant for his troubles; and the war had just ended. Trixie was just 21, the daughter of a coalminer-turned-grocer, and she'd been determined to help the war effort. What did she wear on that night? Who were her girlfriends? Did they drink alcohol? Did the girls huddle together on one side of the hall while the boys stood on the other? There would have been a feeling of buoyancy, celebration and freedom in that hall as the young people let go of what was a pretty horrendous war experience. Their future was rosy and life was good.

The 'haka' must have gone on for a while, because over on the back of the dance card Trixie had written sixteen more musical numbers, again with Arthur featuring frequently, although someone with the initials M.E. made a late run and joined her for a tango. The last dance was a Doris waltz called 'Come and cuddle me', and Arthur got that one.

I watched a few of these dances on YouTube to see exactly what was involved with a Doris waltz or a maxina, and I have to admire my grandparents for what was a lot of skill. All the dances involved being held by your partner and quite a lot of fancy footwork. A far cry from the dancing I did in my youth, which mainly involved jumping up and down on the spot and shaking my head a lot.

Arthur was a very good-looking man. According to his army records, he stood five foot eight inches tall, weighed 131 pounds, had blue eyes, fair hair and a fair complexion. A photo of him that hung on my nana's wall above the TV when I was a child shows a handsome man with a long face, full lips and large, piercing blue eyes, the same as my father's. He was obviously quite a confident sort if he was able to be the master of ceremonies for an army dance.

My grandmother Trixie was also outgoing. She was a wonderful contralto singer who was involved in amateur dramatics and belonged to choirs most of her life. There is a picture of her on my sunroom wall where she is dressed up in a green milk-maid's outfit, complete with a massive matching green bow on her head. She is aged about nineteen, has dark brown eyes, and her hair is tied up so that it looks like she has a bob. She is perched on a tree stump, obviously in character for some musical. Another picture of her shows a much younger girl, with a bow mouth, perky nose and deep brown eyes shaped by thin eyebrows. She wears a Victorian-style white blouse and looks a little startled, but stunning. Think Katherine Mansfield but softer and more innocent-looking.

• • •

Arthur had signed up to fight at the age of eighteen, just weeks after war was declared on 5 August 1914. Legally you had to be nineteen, but he was only three and a half months off his nineteenth birthday so either he lied or they just let him in, figuring that he would be the right age after he had done his training. He didn't leave New Zealand until April 1916 and was sent straight to the Flanders region to be trained in grenades, trench warfare and machine-gunnery as well as being equipped with a gas mask and taught how to use it. He then spent the next three months guarding a 'quiet' sector of the line at Armentières in France, before marching south in September to the Somme battlefields and his first large-scale action on the Western Front.

What ensued over the next 23 days was a fierce and bloody battle, characterised by unrelenting artillery barrages, poison-gas shelling, attacks and counter-attacks, not to mention the harsh living conditions of the trenches which left the men mud-caked, sleep-deprived and shivering. By early October, 2011 New Zealand men had been killed at the Somme. We've all seen it in the movies. Dishevelled, damp, muddy men huddled in trenches with rats, smoking damp cigarettes, then on the call climbing up out of them and running hell for leather at the enemy armed with a bayonet rifle, a couple of grenades, a shovel and a water bottle.

Arthur must have fought well, because his army record sees him taking on the role of Acting Sergeant several times during this period, although it would not be until May 1918 that he was finally promoted to Sergeant.

Arthur's next battle after the Somme was the capture of Messines, where he was wounded in June 1917. It was a bullet to the left thigh, which left a magnificent scar my father can remember seeing as a child; Arthur was also suffering from the effects of being gassed, which meant a slow recovery. Following gas exposure, recovery required weeks of hospitalisation, incapacitating large numbers of soldiers for long periods of time. This was what happened to Arthur. He spent most of the rest of 1917 at Brocton Camp, where he qualified as an instructor. Although he missed the disastrous battle at Passchendaele, he was back in Belgium in November 1917 for the attack at Polderhoek. Finally, at the end of 1918 he went back to France to his final wartime job — the capture of Le Quesnoy, which had been in German hands since 1914. Then it was back to Brocton Camp to wait for a troopship home.

Living near the camp was the woman who would capture Arthur's heart before Trixie. She was 25-year-old Elizabeth Godwin, whose father was a financial manager. Elizabeth was a clerk. Arthur fell in love with her, probably while he was recuperating at Brocton Camp in 1917. Just after he was promoted to Sergeant, Arthur married Elizabeth on 24 July 1918. He was just 23; she was 26.

Arthur planned to take Elizabeth back with him to New Zealand, and he made sure that his army records reflected his new married status. Elizabeth's name and address at Rose Cottage, Weeping Cross, Staffordshire, appear on Arthur's war records in several places.

I'm not sure whether Arthur moved in with Elizabeth after their wedding day and commuted to the camp to work as an instructor. But I do know that he was at Rose Cottage three months later. Shortly after their wedding day, the 1918 flu swept through Europe — including through Brocton Camp, where it killed many of the soldiers stationed there.

Elizabeth came down with the flu, too. She died of double pneumonia on 30 October, just three months after her marriage. Her death certificate records the fact that Arthur was present at her death at Rose Cottage.

On 19 December 1918, a month after the war ended, my grandfather was promoted to Warrant Officer class II, the second-highest rank a non-commissioned soldier could have. He was also made Command Sergeant Major. The dance where he trotted around the floor with Trixie and carried out his duties as MC was just four months after his wife Elizabeth had died.

Long after this manuscript had been handed in to my publishers, I was ferreting around in an old drawer looking for photos of my family for the book designer. In that drawer was an old autograph book, falling to pieces. I had seen it before and always assumed it belonged to one of my parents, but this time I picked it up and was astonished to see that it had Trixie's name and address on the inside leaf and that it was full of mementoes from her friends at Brocton Camp during the war. I was holding a book that my grandmother had held dear more than 100 years ago.

I flicked through it, reading some of the funny verses left by her friends, looking at some lovely sketches and drawings — and then I came across a familiar signature: 'CSM Nissen AG'.

Arthur had written in Trixie's autograph book! Not only that, he had written in it on 30 March 1918, a full year before the haka dance when I had presumed they met.

Arthur wrote:

Take the bitter with the sweet,
The unknown with the known,
As we all must do in life,
Unless we wish to live and die alone.

Then he had added:

Yesterday is but a dream, tomorrow only a vision, but today well
lived makes every yesterday a dream of happiness, and every
tomorrow a dream of hope.

Both are quite well-known proverbs but I remain impressed with my grandfather's entry, being a level above the usual 'roses are red, violets are blue' standard.

So Arthur and Trixie knew each other well before the haka dance and before Arthur married his first wife, Elizabeth, in July 1918. He must have been involved with Elizabeth when he wrote these words for my grandmother, five months before his wedding.

• • •

My dad, Cedric, never knew any of this information about his father until I told him while I was writing this book. He had spent his whole life believing a rumour that his father had been married twice, and thought that there were probably half-brothers and half-sisters out there somewhere — and that his father was perhaps a bigamist.

His mother never talked of his father's earlier marriage, but she knew about it because on their marriage certificate Arthur is described as a widower and his widow's name is on the certificate. But then, Nana never talked about her family; or her husband's family, for that matter. Dad had no idea that he had two maternal uncles in England until a few years ago, when a cousin died in the Isle of Wight and left him a little money.

• • •

A year after the 'haka' at Brocton Camp, Trixie got on a ship called the *Mahana*, heading to Wellington, New Zealand to marry Arthur. She was 22. Trixie left behind her parents George and Mary Ann Mordue as well as three sisters and two brothers. She would never see them again and would have little to do with them. She was the eldest daughter, and there seems to have been some negative feelings about her jumping on a ship to the colonies to marry a man she met in the war. Handsome though he was, and a Warrant Officer to boot, I'm sure her family didn't

DAD, THE QUIET ONE

want to lose their eldest child to New Zealand.

Dad remembers Nana packing up blocks of butter and cheese into kerosene cans which she carefully covered in calico and stitched up to send to her sisters during World War II. He never heard her mention her brothers.

Trixie enjoyed her voyage out to New Zealand on the *Mahana*. She left Liverpool on 27 May 1920 and then found herself stranded onboard ship in Panama City for three weeks. She described this time to my father as one long party. Which was just as well.

When the boat docked in Wellington, Trixie stepped off it full of anticipation for her life with handsome Arthur. She could not have imagined how tough it would be. Arthur had arrived back on the troop ship *Giessen*, which docked in Wellington on 26 August 1919. By September that year, he was living and working with his older brother Fredrick Nissen in Mataroa, North Taihape. I know this because tucked into his army records is a letter written by my grandfather to the Defence Department to inform them of his change of address. He writes:

Bunnythorpe,
23rd Sept 1919

Sir,
I hereby inform you of my intention of changing my address.
I am accepting employment with my brother at Mataroa near

> *Taihape and will be at that place until Christmas at least so if*
> *at any time I am wanted the address given below will find me.*
> *I am leaving Bunnythorpe on Saturday.*
> *I remain Sir,*
>
> *Your Obedient Servant*
> *18595 CSM Nissen AG.*

When I found this letter I took it over to my father's cottage. He looked at the letter and got a bit emotional, seeing his father's handwriting for the first time in his life.

Being a journalist, Dad has always been very particular about grammar. He was delighted to see that his father used a capital 'C' for Christmas. Arthur's determination to do the right thing and inform the Defence Force of his whereabouts indicates a personality trait of obeying the rules. Something my father is very good at as well.

Unfortunately, just two months later Arthur would be discharged from the army as he was 'no longer physically fit for war service'. He had a wound to his left arm, no doubt from sawmilling. I would later find that he had, in fact, had his left ring finger amputated.

Trixie married Arthur on 24 July 1920 at the Ashhurst registrar's office in the Manawatū. Arthur's profession was listed as 'sawmiller.' In the 1920s this was quite a popular thing to do if you were a fit young man. Stands of native trees were common, and for a fee you could purchase a stand, get your equipment and your team in there and drag out the much-sought-after timber for building houses. Arthur was prone to accidents in his new job. Trixie told Dad about having to drag him around on a blanket in the house after a log rolled on top of him and broke both his legs in June 1924. He was also known as the 'saw doctor' because he could fix anything, including the massive saws used in sawmilling.

For the next 15 years following their marriage, my grandparents would move around to various towns in central North Island where Arthur would work as a sawmiller, at one stage owning his own business, and also working as a farmer for a while. My grandmother's early life in New Zealand reminds me strongly of the Jane Campion movie *The Piano*. Having been whirled around the dance floor by handsome Arthur and partied hard during her three-week stopover in Panama, Trixie arrived to life in a tent in the middle of the bush while her husband chopped down trees. She insisted on having a piano, in the tent, in the bush. I'm sure she figured that if they could get a huge kauri tree out of the bush they could get a little piano in.

One can only imagine what a shock it was to this poor woman who had grown up in Durham, a coalmining town in the north-east of England. Her father was a coalminer who then became a grocer, and while their housing was crowded — think Coronation Street and those terraced brick houses — it was comfortable compared with living in the bush. Trixie lived just a three-hour train trip away from London, and was always beautifully turned out and rather stylish. Now she was in the middle of New Zealand, in the middle of the bush, in a tent for god's sake. But even though her life was reduced to such a basic level of living in tents and huts, she kept playing the piano.

Tragically, Trixie had a stillbirth in 1921, just a year after she and Arthur married. She then gave birth to their daughter Beatrice (also called Trixie) on 27 December 1922. Five years later a son, Arthur, was born in June 1927, and then my father Cedric Mordue (Nana's maiden name) on 3 October 1932.

• • •

I pause here to note a picture that my dad found, while I was writing this, of his father in full horse-riding gear — jodhpurs, tie, shirt and boots. He looks for all the world like an English gentleman about to mount his horse for the hunt. He looks fantastic. But in the background is an old water tank, and you realise that this was a one-off, maybe a special race day organised in the local community.

Giving the photo to me, Dad said, 'I've just remembered Mum and Dad had a horse they were very proud of. It was black.' Dad's childhood memories are like that: few and far between.

I like to imagine Arthur in his finery, accompanied by Trixie in hers, heading off to the races that day. For all they knew there would be many more horses and race days and finery to be enjoyed.

Dad spent the first three years of his life living in Te Urewera, deep in the bush. That was a fairly impressive lifestyle for Arthur and Trixie to have led. Even in these modern times, a drive through Te Urewera leaves you with a distinct impression of how rugged and remote the area is. In the 1920s, mills were set up in the bush, with the men and their families living alongside in very primitive conditions. No piped water, no power, no sewers, and no sealed roads. This meant that my nana had to cook over a fire, and was possibly milking a cow and dealing with the men — hard-working Kiwi men, probably ex-soldiers like Arthur. They used axes and saws to fell the trees; this was long before the invention of the chainsaw. Once the timber was felled, the mill moved on.

Te Urewera is rainforest, so it was wet a lot of the time and it could also be cold, very cold. My father says it used to be described as 'cold as a witch's tit'. It has been known to snow in Te Urewera in the summer, so I can imagine that on a cold, wet day in the middle of winter with three kids running around — not to mention the pregnancies — it would have been a tough call for Nana just to get the clothes dry let alone find time to play the bloody piano. I wonder if she ever thought she might have been better off staying back in England in the relative comfort of a proper house with electricity and heating, working for her dad in the grocery shop and marrying the guy down the road.

Dad says Nana was tough and determined, and a little stubborn. Nothing seemed to faze her and she was a hard worker, so those character traits must have helped her through.

I do know that my grandparents were unusually liberal for the era and not at all racist, just like my dad has always been. When I asked Dad why he thought they were so liberal for the times, he explained that Arthur worked with Māori in the bush and there was never any suggestion that there was any difference between them and him, because there wasn't.

The family moved out of the bush around Dad's third birthday because Arthur started feeling unwell and could no longer keep up the active work of the bush. He was 40 years old, and was succumbing to a disease he had caught during the war in France. Syphilis.

CHAPTER 9

Growing up fatherless

As I was writing this chapter, my dad came over for the weekly roast dinner we have at our house. I started prodding him for memories, something which had become quite common for poor old Dad as I wrote the book. An 87-year-old man being interviewed by his daughter constantly is not something many people would enjoy. But he quite liked it.

'I spent my life pushing away anything to do with my dad because it was all so shameful. My mother never talked about him, or mentioned him again after he went away. We never told anyone about it, so I never mentioned my dad to anyone, even you kids.'

Let's not forget that Dad spent his whole life believing that this man had another wife somewhere and was a bigamist.

'Now these memories are flooding back and I'm rather enjoying them. It feels good to be thinking about my dad at last.'

• • •

Like many soldiers on the Western Front in World War I, Arthur may have had a fling, possibly his first, with a French prostitute and later noticed that something wasn't quite right 'down there'. Or, as seems more likely from what I found in his medical records, he may have been exposed to a syphilis sore while in a military hospital. It is thought that at least 16,000 New Zealand soldiers contracted syphilis while in Europe for that war.

Arthur may not have realised he had caught the disease, as the initial symptoms are often relatively minor. At the time there was no cure for syphilis; that would not be available until after World War II, when penicillin was widely used.

In the early years of World War I, before Arthur got to Europe, the army warned soldiers about venereal disease and held regular 'dangle parades' to check their genitals for symptoms. Safer-sex measures like the use of condoms were not mentioned, as this was seen as encouraging immorality. But from late 1917, prophylactic (preventative) kits, devised by Christchurch woman Ettie Rout and containing calomel ointment, condoms and Condy's crystals, were given to men going on leave; they had to take one.

It is interesting to note that New Zealand was the only Allied country to introduce compulsory safe-sex kits for its troops. In 1918, Rout organised a brothel for New Zealanders and Australians in Paris, Madame Yvonne's, where kit use was compulsory. All of this would have been too late for Arthur, because after his injury in June 1917 he spent most of the rest of the war in hospitals or teaching soldiers back at Brocton Camp, away from the front lines. So we have to presume that he contracted the disease soon after arriving in Europe in 1916, or slightly later while he spent a year in hospital.

I liked to think that Arthur didn't know he had syphilis. He might have noticed a painless sore and a rash while knee-deep in mud in the trenches and thought nothing of it, given the conditions. After that initial stage, there are no more symptoms for years. I have chosen to believe this because it means that he would have come home to New Zealand, married the lovely, dainty, stylish, beautiful Trixie Mordue and had a happy life with their three children for the next few decades. Syphilis is not contagious during the latent stage, which he was then in, and there are no indications that it is in the body until the latent stage ends, which can take decades. I want the couple to have got on with their lives — toughing it out in the bush, milling timber, but without the cloud of syphilis hanging over them. Later I would find out that this was indeed true. Neither of them had the faintest idea that Arthur was carrying this lethal disease.

• • •

Syphilis was seen as a major social failing by the soldiers who caught it: they were blamed for not taking precautions, even though many had no idea that precautions were needed. No one seemed to be at all sympathetic about these young men contracting a disease that would, eventually, kill them. Instead it was never, ever talked about. When Arthur finally succumbed to the disease, he became very unwell. Dad remembers his father being sick in bed a lot at this stage; then, when Dad was just seven years old, his father would disappear from his life.

The first symptom Arthur had in this late stage of syphilis was being grandiose, which means that someone has affectations of grandeur or splendour. He had what was clinically called dementia paralytica, a mental disorder caused by meningoencephalitis in late-stage syphilis. This affects seven per cent of those infected with the disease. These symptoms first appear 10 to 30 years after infection and cause fatigue, headaches, insomnia and dizziness. As the disease progresses, mental deterioration and personality changes occur. Sufferers can become grandiose, melancholic or paranoid. Delusions are common, and include ideas of great wealth, immortality, thousands of lovers, unfathomable power, apocalypsis, nihilism, self-guilt, self-blame or bizarre hypochondriacal complaints.

Syphilis took more than 20 years to catch up with Arthur, but when it did he displayed all of the above.

• • •

When I received the 140 pages of my grandfather's medical records from his time in Tokanui Psychiatric Hospital, the woman who had helped me retrieve them rang to say that she was about to email them to me, and told me they were the loveliest records she had ever handled; she got a bit emotional as she said this.

When I looked at them I could see why. They were filled with handwritten letters from my grandmother constantly inquiring about the health of her husband, whether he was getting better and when he would come home. The first of those letters was written just three days after he was admitted:

Dear Sir,

Will you please inform me what you think of my husband's condition as I am very worried about him.

He has always been a good husband and father and it is terrible for this to happen.

I have filled in the forms to the best of my ability but as I did not meet him until the end of 1918 I cannot answer all the questions.

Thanking you in anticipation of an early reply.

Yours faithfully,
MB Nissen

On the afternoon of 7 March 1940 my grandmother had had to make the heartbreaking decision to take her husband to the

Rotorua Police Station. About five months earlier he had been seen by a doctor when he was 'emotional and neurotic'. Now he was out of control.

A doctor called by the police wrote:

His wife says that he has been getting into a more and more drained mental state during recent months and that she is frightened of him.

He was discharged from Social Security work yesterday (because of his statements of grandeur) and refused to cease. When his shovel was taken from him he procured another and continued to work.

Through circumstances he has been working on Scheme 13, and has been living from hand to mouth for some time.

He is perfectly content with life. He says that his wife owns £3000, two working tractors, two working lorries, which bring in £30. He owns 3 million feet of timber which he proposes to sell. He has planned a world tour through America, Africa and England. He also says that he is employed in the Secret Service and has knowledge about the war from Russia, Germany and France and that his number in the Secret Service is 27K.

My grandmother had to admit Arthur to the Tokanui Psychiatric Hospital the next day, under the Mental Defectives Act of 1911. In the forms she had to complete she stated that 'He makes statements to me which are wild and contrary to fact. For example he told me that a local man had shot his wife and children which is not true. He stares at the children with a peculiar look. He makes grandiose statements that he is worth a great deal of money which is contrary to fact.'

My father and his two siblings were told by Trixie that their father had gone to the hospital because of the adverse effects of being gassed during the war. Trixie had no idea that he was suffering from syphilis and was not told of this for many years. Instead, she laboured under the belief that he had suffered a mental breakdown caused by his experience in World War I and the beginning of World War II, which brought it all back to him. She lived in hope that he would be returned to her at some point in the future.

• • •

A few days after that first letter, a return letter from the medical superintendent informed Trixie that Arthur had settled and was behaving well but retained his ideas of grandeur.

From then on, Nana wrote letter after letter, which together make heartbreaking reading. She desperately tries to find a reason why her husband is mentally ill. She suggests that it might be linked to the time he broke his legs, or when he was hit on the head nine years earlier. She asks why he can't come home. She also pleads with the medical superintendent to send the correct paperwork to social security so that she can get a benefit. 'I am in urgent need.'

At the time Arthur was admitted, World War II had been going for a year and New Zealanders were feeling the effects financially. Trixie had no income and three children to care for. She must have been terribly upset and increasingly desperate.

The medical superintendent of the psychiatric hospital showed her little regard, following the practice of the medical establishment at the time which thought it better not to tell people a patient's true medical condition, especially not the wives. Not long after Arthur's admission, in April, Trixie was told that investigations were complete and Arthur was about to commence the appropriate treatment. The doctors knew he had syphilis six days after his admission to the hospital — in his file there is a dated copy of his blood test showing the positive result in red ink and underlined. They knew it meant a slow, mentally disabled crawl to death. But they didn't tell Trixie this, leaving her with the expectation that he would get better and come home.

Her letters reflect an increasing sense of worry and despair. In May 1940 she wrote:

Can you please give me some information about my husband. What do you think of his condition now? And how long do you think it will be before he can come home? In the letter I received from him he seems anxious to come home.

*Until yesterday I had not had a letter from him for a
month and I was very worried. Has he had a relapse
or something?*

She was told that he would be having treatment for the next two
months. Meanwhile, the same man was writing to the Social
Security Department to say that there was no way Arthur would
be discharged in the next twelve months.

It seems that Arthur was quite happy at Tokanui. At the time
it was set out as a pleasant villa with gardens and parks, much
like you see in historical dramas of the period set in Britain
where mentally ill people were sent to rest. The hospital was
self-sufficient in its early days, with its own farm, bakery, laundry,
and even a sewing room where patients' clothes were made. At
its peak in the 1960s there were over a thousand patients living
in the hospital. Records show that Arthur was sleeping well,
eating well, keeping good health generally and enjoying his time
working in the garden. His only problem was causing fights at
meal times because of his grandiose claims. His notes say:

*Conduct good. Employed garden gang. Habits clean. Personal
cleanliness good. Good worker, but very quarrelsome with
other patients.*

In 1942 Trixie was still trying to find a reason for her husband's
illness:

*He had innumerable shrapnel wounds in the war, do you
think it likely that there may be a piece situated somewhere,
causing pressure and this causing the trouble? I am sorry
to keep on bothering you, but I have not quite given up
hope that my husband will recover and I still think his
illness is due to the war.*

She was told that, no, it wasn't the war, but more 'an infection
of the blood' which she was welcome to come and discuss with
the doctors. You have to wonder how that doctor could allow
this woman to tear herself to pieces trying to work out why she
had lost her husband, while all the time he knew why and that
her husband would never be coming home. Part of it perhaps
was the stigma of syphilis, but certainly there was a patriarchal
need to prevent the fairer sex knowing important information
about the one she loved.

• • •

That year, poor Trixie also had to get the Rotorua Returned
Soldiers Association involved because the hospital would not
send back an application form for a Veteran's Allowance signed
by Arthur; they said he was unable to sign it. This was at the
same time Arthur was writing quite coherent letters to his wife
in Rotorua. The secretary of the Association wrote:

*My Association is very anxious to do something in this case as
Mrs Nissen had to give up her employment in August last owing
to ill health, and she now only has her pension to live on and it
is not sufficient. I think that if we can get a Veterans' allowance
(which she is entitled to) she will be able to manage.*

At the time my father was aged ten, his brother Arthur
fifteen and his sister Trixie twenty. Dad remembers his sister
working and giving him some pocket money each week to spend
on sweets. But Dad could also buy his own sweets, because since
the age of eight, just a year after his father went to hospital, he
began an after-school job delivering groceries. He worked before
and after school during his entire education, eventually being
employed at the local menswear store where one of his least
enjoyable jobs was turning up at 6 a.m. on a Monday morning to
clean away the vomit and urine left by weekend drunks down an
alleyway by the store. He told me that at one stage he was earning
eight shillings a week, six of which he would give his mother.

Eventually Trixie got the Veteran's Allowance, but only after
a lot of fuss involving the Public Trust because the all-powerful
medical superintendent who was sitting on all those secrets made
a big deal about his belief that Arthur didn't know what he was
signing. What a guy.

By 1943, Trixie was still writing letters to her husband,
sending money, visiting him and writing letters to the medical
superintendent.

*I wish I could do more for him than I am doing but, as
I have only a pension of £7.19.3 per month it is impossible
to do more.*

*I don't like to worry you too much but I am praying
that my husband will some day be restored to health. He
has now been in hospital over three years and the doctor
here thought he would only be away a few weeks and,
my youngest boy especially is always wanting to know
when his father is coming home.*

That was my dad, Cedric, aged 11, just wanting his dad. Around
this time, as Trixie was trying to cope on her pension and her
children's earnings, things started to take a turn for the worse.
Arthur was confined to bed and his health was declining. Trixie
wrote again, offering to come at a moment's notice if he asked
for her, even though because of the war the train service was no
longer running; but perhaps she could get some 'benzine' and
ask a friend to drive her through.

What Trixie didn't know was that Arthur was in a straitjacket
for between 20 and 22 hours a day for three months because
he was covered in boils and was interfering with his dressings.
He was also being given doses of paraldehyde, a sedative that was
commonly used in psychiatric hospitals until the 1970s. These
were bad times for Arthur, but Trixie was none the wiser. She did
start trying to work out how he got this 'infection of the blood'
the hospital was talking about. In a really sad letter she says:

My husband was a most fastidious man and in the time I have known him, a gentleman, both in word and deed. I have recently learned that he was circumcised at Rigley Military Camp in 1918 ...

By October 1944, Trixie had had enough. She decided that she wanted to talk to the doctors herself and get some answers, and so she visited. What she found was a man who no longer knew who she was. 'I have often wondered if perhaps he had not been committed to the institution he might have recovered at home, as he had a horror of hospitals,' she later wrote.

She was also told, finally, about the syphilis. Well, sort of.

You were very good in trying to explain his illness but I am still very puzzled about it. For instance, you say his disease is not hereditary yet you advise me to have my children examined, also myself. As I am not a blood relation of my husband's I cannot understand the reason.

I have not told the children the full extent of their father's illness. They only know he is ill through his injuries at the war. I don't want their lives to be overshadowed.

My grandmother got a telling-off for writing this letter to the doctor concerned and not the medical superintendent. He was really pissed off at the breach of protocol. It was 'explained' that the blood disease was not hereditary but she and her children should get blood tests. If her doctor needed to know anything else he could contact the superintendent. Again, there would be no explanation of the truth for my nana unless it came through a medical officer. They were still unable to say the word 'syphilis', which I find astounding — but believable for the times.

Trixie wrote straight back and explained that she thought it was a good idea to write to the doctor she had seen, as he had been good enough to talk to her, not him, so there. Then came a heartbreaking paragraph; she had seen her local doctor who had decided that enough was enough and had told her the truth.

I am afraid it came as a great shock to me as I had never thought of anything like that. I had a blood test taken yesterday and am praying it may prove negative.

This was 6 July 1944 — over four years since Arthur had been admitted to the mental hospital. Her test was negative.

Dad never visited his father; I'm sure Trixie would have discouraged such visits as she tried to wade her way through her husband's illness and protect her children. He does remember his mother going to visit his father at Tokanui Psychiatric Hospital. She had to take the train from Rotorua to Te Awamutu; the hospital was fourteen kilometres out of town, which would mean either an expensive taxi with money she didn't have or a bus. At the time she was working in a bakery to support the family, so she would have had to make these trips in the weekend when she probably wanted to spend time with her children or perhaps relax a little.

In May 1945, Trixie was still hoping for a recovery. Obviously her local doctor had not quite got around to telling her the bit about the end-stages of syphilis, which would see Arthur become completely incapacitated and bedridden until he died. She wrote to the medical superintendent on 24 May:

> *Will you please inform me how my husband is. In view of the new drugs coming on the market do you think there is any hope of an improvement in his condition?*
>
> *I cannot understand my husband marrying me knowing that he might pass on the disease to me or my children. Do you think he could have had the disease and not known about it?*
>
> *It does not seem possible but knowing my husband as I do I cannot reconcile myself to the idea that he knew he was infected when we were married.*

My grandmother was referring to penicillin, which in 1943 had been found to be effective in treating the early stages of syphilis.

In response, Trixie was told there was no new drug that would repair the damage done to Arthur's mind. But she was also told: 'It is by no means certain that your husband knew that he had contracted the disease. He has certainly denied ever having been infected when we have questioned him and it is not unknown for a person to contract this disease and know nothing about it.'

Trixie kept on praying and hoping and writing to the hospital inquiring after Arthur's health well into 1947, and always received the same standard reply. No improvement — sometimes just said in one sterile, dismal sentence.

She also sent money, pencils, paper and gifts, even though he no longer knew who she was, could not write to her and she could not visit.

• • •

Finally, on 18 March 1948, Arthur George Nissen died, aged 53. According to his death certificate he died of pneumonia, toxaemia, bedsores and dementia paralytica.

I would like to say that the staff at the psychiatric hospital gave my nana plenty of notice and she was able to be with him when he passed away. But again, information was withheld. The local Rotorua police were asked to visit my nana at 8.45 p.m. on the day of my grandfather's death and inform her of it.

She wrote to the hospital five days later:

Dear Sir,

Can you please give me any particulars of my husband's death?
Did he die peacefully and did he get his memory back at all?
I am very grateful for your care of him all these years and had

kept hoping for an improvement in his condition.

Thanking you once again and I am only very sorry I was not informed in time to see him before he died.

In answer she was told that he had been confined to bed for some time, and showed signs of serious deterioration two days before his death. They did say he died peacefully.

As I got to the end of my grandfather's medical records, a more recent letter popped out. It had been written in December 1985 by my aunty Trixie, who would have been about 63 at the time; her mother Trixie was living in a care home by then. My aunt was asking for details of her father's illness, and she knew the year he had been admitted: 1940, when she was aged seventeen. Her father's disappearance must have taken a huge toll on her as she went through her teens helping her mother and her younger brothers. It is obvious from her letter that her mother had never told her of Arthur's illness.

The medical superintendent in 1985 was obviously a much more open and caring fellow than the one my grandmother had dealt with. He wrote my aunty Trixie a long letter which included the information that her father had had positive signs of acquired syphilis which he had contracted many years before, possibly while a patient in a military hospital. Although syphilis is a sexually transmitted disease, you can also get it from being in contact with a syphilis sore, so perhaps this happened in the hospital he was in. This superintendent rather kindly sent the letter to the local senior social worker in my aunt's area, and asked her to hand-deliver it to my aunt rather than callously post it.

My grandmother had spent eight years praying and hoping that her husband would recover and come back to her. Had the medical superintendent at Tokanui Psychiatric Hospital had the courtesy to sit her down early on and tell her that there was no way Arthur would get better or come home, she might have spent those eight years a little differently. She might still have pined and prayed and hoped. But she also might have moved on and had some enjoyment of a life not marred by continuous anxiety. It doesn't really matter whether or not she would have, but it *does* matter that it should have been her right to know, and her choice to decide how to live her life unhindered by one powerful man's determined obfuscation.

• • •

The next month, Trixie was offered her husband's effects, which included slippers, braces and suspenders, a cardigan, trousers, two ties, pyjamas, a coat, fourteen handkerchiefs plus a hairbrush and shaving equipment. She replied that she would take all but the cardigan, braces and suspenders as she had a son aged nearly sixteen, still at school, and these items might come in useful for him. She enclosed postage.

Dad has a vague memory of trying on some shirts that were too small. He was taller than his father, and fit. Later he remembers opening a drawer in his mother's bedroom and being overcome by a familiar smell. It was his father's smell of tobacco, a very pleasant smell he associated with nice times. My nana must have kept those clothes in that drawer and smelled them often.

By the time his father died, Dad was in his teens and by his account spending all his time up at the farm with his mate John. He remembers his mother organising a friend of hers to teach him the piano. Dad is quite musical, like his mum.

To her embarrassment, the piano teacher would turn up and Dad would be nowhere to be found, usually up at the farm helping herd sheep or raiding the sheds looking for eggs to fry up for a feed.

Dad was always told that his father was in hospital because of the gas he was attacked with in the war. It wasn't until he was a teenager that his older brother Arthur told him the real reason their father was no longer living with them, and Dad has had a deep sense of shame about that all his life. So much so that he showed little interest in his father, hid away any memories of him, and never mentioned him.

When Dad and my mother got married, he insisted that they both got tested for syphilis, convinced that if he had it he would pass it on to Mum and his children. He also developed a deep hatred for war, became a pacifist and refused to even watch war movies because they glorified such terrible events. I guess to a seven-year-old child losing your dad because of the war has its effect on you.

When I was writing this chapter, I would head over to Dad's cottage next door and regale him with the information I had found out that day about his dad. Slowly he started recalling memories and sharing them with me. One such memory was of being a toddler in his cot in the bedroom when his father came in to find that somehow Dad had managed to get hold of some sweets and unwrapped them all from their wrappings. He was sitting there, covered in sticky sweets and wrappers. His father just laughed, sat down and gently took each sweet, put it back in its wrapper and carefully wrapped them up again, one by one.

'He was a kind man,' Dad said. 'Never angry or violent.'

He also remembers a trip with his dad and his workmates out to a Māori village near Rotorua when he would have been about four years old. My grandfather must have decided to take his little boy to work that day, and so Dad was in the truck with the workmen. This was in the 1930s during the Depression, and they were building a house. They were probably being paid to do so by the government. Dad can clearly remember his father instructing him to go and knock on a nearby whare and ask the Māori woman for some tea leaves so that they could make themselves some tea. He got a whole cup of tea leaves and his dad was very pleased with him.

That's about it for Dad's memories of his father.

My dad never took me to see Arthur's grave; in fact, I doubt anyone in the family has visited it since the funeral. When I was writing this book I went to find it in Hamilton East cemetery and put some roses on it, roses being his wife's favourite flower. Through writing his story I became very close to Arthur in my head, if that's possible. I felt a bond with him because everything about him seemed to be just like my dad. I wish he had known me as a child, I wish he had lived to see the moon landing, and television and all those things that happened so soon after he died. I know he would have been a lovely grandfather, and my nana would have been so much happier had he lived longer and they had spent more time together.

CHAPTER 10

My Nana Trixie

I knew Nana Trixie until she died when I was 27 with two little kids. She lived to the ripe old age of 92.

When Dad left Rotorua, at the age of eighteen, he knew his mother didn't want him to, but typically for Trixie she never said anything. When he married my mum, Elsie, Trixie wasn't too happy either. I guess that's what happens when your son marries a woman who is also tough, determined and a little stubborn, just like you.

Mum always said Nana had 'airs and graces', but the woman I knew was just British with an accent she never lost, and very stylish. A photo taken at Mum and Dad's wedding in 1954 shows Mum's mother, Olive, looking quite plain in an old woollen coat that was too big for her, smartened up with a corsage, along with wire-rimmed glasses and a hat which had seen better days plonked on her head. She wore no jewellery and her hair was short and curly, probably permed. Nana, on the other hand, wore a sumptuous fur stole over a satin dress with diamanté buttons. She completed the outfit with pearl earrings, a delicate necklace and gloves, and her hair had been styled with a wave. She also wore a hat with beaded netting falling over her face. She was the height of glamour.

The irony of this was that Nana was much poorer than Olive, who had a husband in work, but Trixie put the effort in. She was also, at the time, managing a lady's dress shop in Rotorua, a job that would see her finally able to save enough money to buy a little cottage out on Old Taupo Road in Rotorua. At 57 years old at the time of my parents' wedding she was still a beautiful woman, but there was never anyone else in her life after Arthur.

Eventually Nana would sell her old cottage and move to Auckland to be nearer my dad. She bought another little cottage out in Beach Haven near my parents' home in Birkenhead, which I remember fondly. It had a lemon tree outside the kitchen door which she would feed with her bath water. Her front door was adorned with a climbing rose. Her flower gardens were well tended and she seemed very happy in her little place. This is when I got to know my nana, because she would occasionally take my brother and I for an overnight stay. We would sleep on little divans that Dad had built in her sunroom. The radio was always on 1YC, playing classical music and sometimes show-tunes that she would hum along to while frying rissoles for our dinner in her electric frying pan.

I liked being with Nana because her unique accent and her style fascinated me. She was chatty, and always had something to talk about. She also loved to watch *Coronation Street*, as I did, so we always had that in common. I also had the feeling that she was having us for the night under sufferance. Which is probably fair enough.

When we arrived at Nana's house she would always walk us up to the dairy and buy us some treats, then it was back to her house for rissoles (always), a piece of cake, watching some telly, then off to bed.

Dad would often pick Nana up and bring her back to our house for birthday dinners and family events. She had a special chair that was nice and high so she could get into it easily. She would request a small sherry or a ginger ale and then sit in the chair with her handbag on her lap, sipping her drink ever so sweetly and never saying a word. In old age, the extrovert amateur dramatics singer had developed into an introverted person who really enjoyed her own company — not unlike my father, who now lives happily on his own albeit just through the garage from us.

As Nana got older she began to have falls. Dad would be called by the neighbour to go out and rescue her, which usually involved a hospital admission. One weekend Mum and Dad were away and I got the call at home. I was fifteen and immediately hopped in my car and drove across the bridge from Birkenhead to Auckland Hospital, where I found Nana dazed and confused in Accident and Emergency. I had rung my parents but they were hours away, so I stayed with her through the night, holding her hand and making her cups of tea. It wasn't until my dad turned up in the morning, shocked to see that I was still there, that I realised most fifteen-year-olds might have gone home. It had never occurred to me.

After that, Nana lived with us briefly. I remember it being a time of intense bad feelings between her and my mother, who resented having to look after her. Nana was not at all happy to be there either. Eventually Dad took Nana back to her cottage.

During my later teens I was really close to my nana and would visit her in her cottage frequently. I always made sure I took my boyfriends out to meet her. She must have told me to do this, because it became a rite of passage for them.

'You have to meet my nana before we go any further,' I think I said.

Eventually, she became too frail to live on her own and Dad had to make the awful decision to move her to a care home. 'I never thought you'd be the one to do this to me,' she told him, breaking his heart.

By this time I was busy with my career and raising my two little toddlers. I used to drive by Nana's care home every day on my way to and from work, yet for some reason I never stopped in to see her. I visited her a couple of times, but to my eternal shame I was always just too busy.

Nana remained in rude good health and died at the age of 92. At her funeral my baby daughter Hannah, who we had been keeping quiet in the church service by feeding her grapes, spectacularly threw up all over us. That's my only memory of the funeral, sadly.

Olive Peterson, Mum's adoptive mother, was a kind woman who always had a cigarette in her hand.

Mum's birth mother, Eileen Gallagher (centre), as a young woman. She came knocking on Olive's door not long after the adoption took place, looking for her daughter.

Mum's adoptive parents, Olive (left) and Harold, having a picnic with Mary, who came to live with them and made my mother's life hell.

Mum's childhood often included happy moments, especially with pet animals.

Full house: my mum (centre left) with some of her adoptive siblings.

LEFT: Mum was funny and sharp-witted; you can see it in her eyes here. She's dressed up to play the role of minister at a mock wedding, perhaps for a church or school play. RIGHT: Early evidence of Mum's lady-like side.

Mum with her birth mother, Eileen, outside the house at Whanganui.

LEFT: Nana Trixie (Dad's mother), dressed up in the milk-maid's outfit I describe on page 105. She loved singing and acting. RIGHT: Arthur Nissen married Trixie in July 1920. This is the photo that hung on the wall above Nana's TV when I was a child.

Take the bitter with the sweet,
the unknown with the known,
as we all must do in life,
unless we wish to live and die alone.

"Yesterday is but a dream, tomorrow only a vision, but today well lived makes every yesterday a dream of happiness, and every tomorrow a dream of hope."

E.B.H. Nissen No
N.Z.R.B.
Brocton Camp
Staffs. 30-3-1918

Arthur's entry in Trixie's autograph book, dated 30 March 1918. It was a surprise to me that they knew each other back then, just months before Arthur married his first wife.

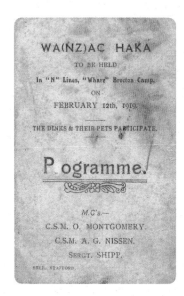
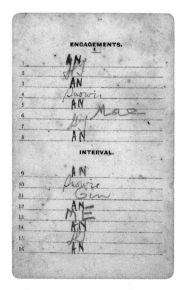

The cover and inside page of Trixie's dance card for the WA(NZ)AC HAKA held on 12 February 1919. Arthur's initials (A.N.) appear numerous times.

LEFT: Trixie gathering fern fronds in Te Urewera bush in the early days of her marriage to Arthur. RIGHT: Nana Trixie dressed up for a day out, in the era when I knew her best.

LEFT: Arthur (Dad's father) kitted out in riding gear. RIGHT: My dad, Cedric, was a dead ringer for his father. As a teenager he competed in swimming and rugby.

LEFT: My parents, Cedric and Elis (then known as Elsie), dressed up for an event. RIGHT: Cedric and Elsie on their wedding day, 6 June 1954.

This is the photo of Olive, Harold and Trixie at my parents' wedding that I talk about on page 139. As always, Nana Trixie is looking super glam.

Mum and me at Northcote Point in Auckland, where I spent my childhood (we moved to Birkenhead when I was eight).

Dinner with friends on our disastrous 2006 holiday — the one I've dubbed the 'slut cruise'. Mum is seated next to me.

LEFT: A happier snap of Mum on the jetty with her beloved dog Pepper.
RIGHT: Mum in the pool with two of her granddaughters, Mariko (left) and my daughter Hannah.

CHAPTER 11

The three sides
of Elis

I knew three Elis Nissens. First there was Nice Elis, the one most people knew. Funny, a great conversationalist, intelligent, well-read, empathetic and sympathetic, eager to help and look after people. She taught English to refugees who would turn up at our home quiet and confused; many of them became lifelong friends. She paid for her friend's daughter to have an abortion in the days when you had to fly to Sydney to get it done, because they had to hide it from the friend's husband. She cuddled kids and babies, and loved all children, including mine and my brother's. She had a 'candle in the window' policy so that her children, and our friends, always knew they could come home when they needed help. She fed and clothed us well, ensured I got braces when I needed them, and managed long family holidays on remote islands in the Hauraki Gulf.

She and Dad cared for one of my nieces for four years when

she was a teenager because things weren't great at home. That's a hell of a thing to do when you are in retirement, taking on a teenager and paying for her upkeep out of your super. I respected my parents for doing this even if, I feel, they were never given much credit for it.

Next there was Lady Elis. You knew that Lady Elis was in the house because she had a lot of make-up on and a lot of jewellery. Her head was held at a different angle to Nice Elis: chin high, mouth pursed. She spoke with a different accent. Some people will remember their mother getting on the phone and 'talking posh' in the old days. Lady Elis talked posh the whole time. She was a terrible snob, a know-all bore and loved to put people down. It was Lady Elis who sometimes appeared to set the table and cook us breakfast.

Then there was Bad Elis. My children learned to identify Bad Elis, and named the peculiar squinting that signalled her appearance as 'lizard eyes'. If you walked into the room and Mum was doing a very good impression of a tuatara, you immediately made plans to get out of there — fast. Bad Elis was plain nasty from start to finish. Instead of 'Hello, how nice to see you' when you came to visit, Bad Elis would say 'Oh, there you are, took your time.' She would then wait until you were seated and comfortable before launching into the latest instalment of 'The Bridge Ladies Say'. This was usually their take on something I had said on the radio or written in a column, or something that had just been made up by The Bridge Ladies.

The attack would last as long as she could draw it out, and you would sit and take it. Then you would get up and leave, gathering your children as you went, hoping they would forget what they had witnessed.

Eventually, when I was 49 and The Bridge Ladies had told her that on the radio I had talked about having my head flushed down the toilet by my mother as a child, I decided that Bad Elis would no longer have an audience.

'You just make up bullshit about your childhood,' she'd spat. 'You are a bare-faced liar.'

I stood up.

'I'm about to turn 50 and I've had enough of this.' I walked out, leaving Paul to gather up the kids and my handbag. We drove home and I felt amazingly free (and brave).

From that day on, if I called in and Bad Elis was in residence, I would drastically shorten the visit on the spot.

'Look, I'm sorry I'm not here for long, I've just popped in on my way to somewhere,' I would say.

I could get in and out in two minutes, my father standing by the whole time — understanding, I think. I would sometimes feel bad about leaving him to cope with Bad Elis, but then I realised he had made a choice to live with that Elis so I was sure he had his own strategies for coping.

The day after I first walked out on Bad Elis, I wondered if there would be a call to talk it through, make amends, reach a compromise. But of course there wasn't. In my mother's book, if you don't acknowledge that something bad has happened, then it never happened.

• • •

There was no rhythm or frequency to the appearance of Mum's three personalities. They just turned up whenever. Which made it tough to negotiate, but negotiate you did. As a child I knew these personalities intimately but thought they were normal. For all I knew, all mothers had three personalities. Some days Mum had some wines, told jokes and was great fun. I loved that Mum. Some days she was just plain nasty and hard to live with; eventually she would take herself off to her bed to sleep, and I would take off to a friend's house or one of my many after-school saviour activities. And some days, Lady Elis would be wafting around doing a very good impression of Hyacinth Bucket from the BBC show *Keeping Up Appearances* and it was vaguely entertaining.

One Saturday, I sat down at my sewing machine and miraculously worked a piece of bright yellow jersey silk into a halter-neck maxi dress. It was gorgeous, with two triangles of fabric coming up from the waistband to cover my breasts. It would be fair to say that my breasts were poached eggs and barely filled the triangles, but it was 1974 and flat chests were making a stand. I was twelve, tall and skinny, and put the dress on together with my wooden platform sandals to wear that night because Mum and Dad were having friends over for a party. I was passing around cheese straws, as all good middle-class daughters did in those days, and could tell that people were looking at me. It was a good feeling, a feeling that made me feel I was attractive. Then I heard my mother's voice: 'Look at my daughter — she doesn't have any tits!' There was an uncomfortable silence as everyone focused on my tiny breasts. I left the room and sat down on my bed in my bedroom. Then I got up and walked out again, back into the room full of people. Fuck you, Mum, I thought. You're not going to win this.

Things got tough when I became a teenager because I answered back and was no longer under Mum's control. When my brother and I had a party when Mum and Dad were away one weekend, I got the blame.

'You promised us that you wouldn't have a party while we were away,' Mum said during the telling-off, which involved my father sitting there uncomfortably, saying nothing.

'So what? I lied,' I replied, then got up and walked out, hopped in my car and drove to a friend's house for the night.

Early on I realised that it was best not to be in the house if Dad wasn't there. My brother was quite rough and would often chase me up and down the house, and then administer a punch or a kick — just enough to hurt, not enough to scar or bruise. I knew this was common in many households where there were teenage boys, I had seen it at friends' houses so I put up with it. One Saturday morning the chase was on, but Dad was home and was horrified at what he had just witnessed.

'You never, ever hit a woman!' he shouted at my brother, red-faced and clearly angry (which was a rare thing to see in my father).

This was when I set about planning my after-school activities to keep me out of the house between the end of school and Dad getting home around 6 p.m. Mondays I did piano lessons, Tuesdays ballet class, Wednesdays tennis or athletics, Thursdays ballet class, Fridays work at the chemist shop down the road. I knew on a very basic level that shit wasn't great, but I was doing okay at school, had lots of friends and seemed to be coping.

Years later, my mother would tell me she knew exactly what I was doing with all my after-school activities. She knew I was avoiding her. I just looked at her and wondered if an apology was about to come, or an acknowledgement of how horrible it all was, but nothing ever came. Mum never apologised for any of her actions. Sorry is a word I never heard my mother say.

When Mum was down, she seemed to find it comforting to tease me. Relentlessly. Often my brother joined in on these sessions, which made fun of my hair, my body, my clothes, my piano playing, my ballet ability, my intelligence. It was all fair game.

I once stood my ground on this and demanded to know why she needed to be so mean about me. Her response was to tell me to 'toughen up'. She explained that I needed to develop a thick skin to survive in this world. I'm sure this was exactly the way she was spoken to in her own childhood. I did 'toughen up', though I'm not really sure I needed to. I can take all sorts of abuse, churn it around in my head and spit it out right back at the poor person who thought it might upset me. I don't regard this as a great skill to have, however, because it came at a huge cost to me as a child.

CHAPTER 12

Not normal

Mum liked to tell a story of how she fooled Dad in the early days of their marriage in Wellington. They had a disagreement, and she walked out of the house. Dad got worried when she didn't return and hopped in their car — spending most of the night driving around Wellington looking for her. After a while he returned home, and as he was parking the car she popped up from the back seat where she had been hiding the whole time. She thought this was hilarious as a story, but I know Dad never saw the funny side.

When I was about fourteen, things got really bad with Mum due to some rather large problems with my parents' marriage which I would overhear being worked through every night. I would put my ear to the wall using a glass, as I had seen on television programmes, and hear my parents arguing. At first it was fascinating, then it was scary, and then it was so horrible

I stopped listening and put my head under the pillow so I couldn't hear anymore. My mother was a cruel and punishing arguer.

I would often spend time crying my eyes out with my best friend Samantha on the school playing field. Finally I decided to visit our family doctor because I felt very strongly that my mother needed help and I wanted to find out what I could do.

Our family doctor was a groovy guy who drove a sports car and had permed hair. 'Funky' is a good word to describe this 1970s purveyor of Valium whom my mother worshipped. She even bought his sports car off him.

I booked in to see him after school in Milford, and walked there from Westlake Girls' High School. I went into his surgery and told him of my mother's sadness, the hours spent in the bedroom, the irrational behaviour, and how I was frightened for her — and for me, to be honest. His response was disappointing. He said he couldn't tell me anything about my mother's health because of patient confidentiality. Unbelievably, he sent me away with nothing. No advice, no suggestion that I seek help from a trusted friend or relative, or any reassurance that things were alright. Nor did he bother to contact my parents and tell them that their fourteen-year-old daughter was so concerned about the mental health of her mother that she had come to see him.

A while later, when I was fifteen, I went back to see our funky doctor to get the contraceptive pill, and made a point of reminding him of that patient confidentiality and his need to not tell my parents.

• • •

I gave birth to my first child, Daniel, in the middle of winter on 28 July 1986. What followed was an extremely lonely period in a cold, dark house in Avondale, with very little money and my boyfriend at work all day. My mother arrived once a week in full make-up and jewellery, together with a friend, and sat in the lounge waiting for morning tea. I would serve them tea while they watched my beautiful baby squirm and wriggle on the floor. I was 24, looked a fright and had no idea what I was doing. After an hour she would leave, having not lifted a finger to do anything except drink her tea. I would spend the afternoon in tears, wondering how to cope with my tiny baby boy. Two weeks later, my boyfriend's mother, Antoinette, drove up from Tauranga and moved in to help me. I was suffering from post-natal depression and wasn't coping; anyone could see that — just not my mother. This was normal for her.

My third child, Virginia Marguerite Nissen Ellison, died of cot death on 28 June 1992. As her father and I grieved for our baby and tried to cope with our two other children, my mother sat in our lounge and demanded tea. I made it for her, and then she said: 'This is the worst thing that has ever happened to me.' She left, once more having not lifted a finger to do anything except drink her tea. I followed her to the door and said to my father: 'Don't bring her back here. I can't look after her as well.' Again, shortly afterwards my now mother-in-law Antoinette moved in to help me. When she made tea for the grief counsellor who came to visit, she pulled out my best china teacups. I loved her for that.

It was always my fault when I needed to get away from Elis, not hers; I was a bad daughter. Even when I was in my early forties, I was still succumbing to this sort of brainwashing by my mother.

After a period of not talking to my mother for a few years, I decided it was time to make amends. I bought her a ticket on a cruise around the Pacific with me for ten days. On day two, we joined some people we knew at a table for dinner. My hair had been blow-dried at the ship's salon, and I was wearing a short dress with tassels on the bottom. It was 2006 and that was very fashionable. As I walked back to the table after going to the toilet during dinner, my mother looked at me and said, 'Look at my daughter, the big slut.' There was silence. The other two women didn't know what to say. Later, one of them said she was so shocked. 'I had no idea Elis could be so nasty. I've never seen that side of her before. Does it happen often?'

I sat down and got on with dinner. Fuck you, Mum. The rest of the cruise involved daily abuse of this nature, which I just couldn't understand, and still don't. When the ship docked back in Auckland I went one way with Paul and she went the other with my father. I didn't talk to her for another year.

• • •

I did get some counselling about my childhood but not until I was quite old — about 44, just after the disastrous slut cruise.

We identified Elis's three personalities, and it was explained to me that this might not be a major mental illness with a convenient name to label it with. It might just be a coping mechanism that Mum had developed over the years to deal with the various awful things that had happened to her as a child, reflecting the way she had been treated.

And then I was told that my mother was an alcoholic and was jealous of me. Both of these things I rejected.

'Mum likes a drink, but she's not an alcoholic,' I replied.

'Have you ever seen her go a day without a drink, and not drink until she falls asleep?' said my counsellor.

'God, no! Mum always drinks, but it's social drinking,' I said, repeating my mother's own explanation for her love of booze.

Mum would often say, 'I'm going to get high tonight!', whether she was celebrating something or was sad about something. 'Getting high' was her daily dose of self-medication. As a child, I would see her take a glass flagon of sherry, still in its paper bag, out from under the sink and have a good swig while cooking dinner. Several times. I thought everyone's mother did this. Before she joined Dad for pre-dinner drinks when he got home from work, she would have been high alright.

'Why don't you try limiting your phone calls and dealings with your mum to the morning and early afternoon, before she starts drinking?' my counsellor suggested.

It worked like a charm. No more Bad Elis or Lady Elis appearances. Just Nice Elis.

As for the jealousy, my response was one of horror. As the mother of daughters, I couldn't imagine ever feeling jealous of them in any way. How could you look at your beautiful, successful daughter and not feel anything but immense love and pride, and tell her so? That's so wrong. But then what happened to my mother as a child was also very wrong.

'Why, then, do you think she never lets you talk to your father or have a relationship with him?'

My counsellor was right. Whenever my father answered the phone, it was physically snatched away from him by my mother within seconds.

'But I wanted to talk to Dad,' I would say.

'What have you got to say to him that you can't say to me?' she would reply.

As a child, Dad and I had three things we were allowed to do together, just the two of us. One was fishing on a Sunday morning when I was little, one was peering under the bonnet of a car and fiddling with engines, and the other was watching television together when Mum was out at a Weight Watchers meeting in the evening. I loved snuggling up to him on the couch and having time just with him. He liked it, too.

My counsellor continued: 'Why does she need to put you down in front of other people?'

I had no idea.

'Your mother has difficulty dealing with your success and uses these devices to help her feel better, even though they are cruel to you.'

I thought about every achievement I had had in my life and realised that each was met with a very lukewarm response from Mum. She was a big supporter of the Kiwi 'don't get a big head' school, and constantly told me not to get above myself. When I was given the editorship of *Woman's Day* magazine (the biggest-selling women's mag in the country) at the age of 30, when I was still in the middle of grieving the death of my daughter less than a year before, her reaction was one of immediate scorn.

'Why couldn't you have got *Metro* magazine instead of that trash? I'll certainly never put it on *my* coffee table for people to see.'

That led to the one and only fight my first husband ever had with my mother. He told her she was a mean old bag and stormed out of the house.

My mother had never said 'I love you' or 'I'm proud of you'.

'What mother can't say she loves her daughter or that she is proud of her?' I asked myself. A jealous one.

• • •

The first time I pulled away from my mother was when I was seventeen and studying to be a journalist. Bad Elis had been in the house for several days, and I had recently returned from a year in the United States as an exchange student, which I had done as a way of leaving home before I legally could. I knew that it was quite nice not being around Mum. I left to live with a friend down the road and cut myself off from my mother completely.

During that year, my dad would ring once a week to check up on me, and would frequently meet me for lunch and offer me money if I needed it. I knew he was doing this without my mother knowing and would pay a huge price if she found out. I also knew that it meant my dad loved me unconditionally, which was important to me and, I think, helped me deal with a lot of things later in life. If you have a parent who is there for you through thick and thin, then you have a solid foundation of love.

What amazed me was that for a whole year my mother never made an effort to make amends. Not a note or a phone call to her seventeen-year-old daughter, who was working nights at the Hungry Horse restaurant to pay her rent and studying during the day. Not. One. Call. I would die if I couldn't talk to one of my kids for a day, let alone a year, and would never let a disagreement last longer than a few hours before talking it over. I was their mother, and my job was to help them through whatever it was they were struggling with.

That year ended when I had my first depressive episode and was delivered back to my parents by a caring and concerned boyfriend. My mother loved me when I was down. I saw it at the time as her being a caring, loving person, but later in life, during counselling, I realised that when I was down she felt great, because she could be superior and not feel any jealousy at all for the pathetic creature huddled on her couch, unable to eat or function properly.

After a week or two of being down, I would feel better. Bad Elis would return and I'd head off again, until the next time I stumbled and fell back into the arms of Nice, unthreatened, Elis.

. . .

I believe that we are all wired differently, and within the same family one child might be badly affected by some bad parenting while another seems to cope. I was definitely the coper in my family dynamic, and very much managed to get on with my life despite my mother's strange parenting. I also made up my mind not to pass any of her parenting on to my children, as often happens.

I have never, ever criticised or discussed the clothes my children wear, which was often challenging, believe me.

I have never shamed my children or made them feel uncomfortable about who they are.

I have never sulked or created a mood of anger in my home so that they needed to walk on eggshells for days on end.

I have never allowed a disagreement to brew, and have worked hard to keep a good line of communication with my children.

I have always been there for them, in good times and in bad.

This does not mean that I have been the perfect parent. Alcohol was a problem for a while, and I know this was unpleasant for my family. And sometimes I lost my temper and shouted. But mostly, I was not my mother. Ever.

CHAPTER 13

Dementia calling

I n late November 2016, Mum's doctor wrote in her medical file: 'Elis thinks she needs more meds, says not thinking clearly, bit fuzzy headedness. Husband gets fed up with her forgetfulness. Says she doesn't take oxazepam every day.'

When you are in your eighties it is easy to think that the early signs of dementia are just old age. Feeling fuzzy-headed and forgetting things is something most people do as they get older. But for Mum it was bad enough for her to go to her doctor and ask for some pills to make it go away.

Mum was a great believer in the power of pharmaceuticals and had been her whole life. She was from the generation that put its faith in the local GP and was quite happy to swallow whatever pill they advised. Feel bad. Go to doctor. Get pill. Feel better. That was the recipe for good health, which was understandable for her generation. In my mother's lifetime, major advances had been made in curing diseases that were very active in her child-hood. Polio had gone. TB had gone. Syphilis had gone. When your life has been spent observing the birth and celebration of vaccines and pharmaceuticals that save lives, you learn to trust them. These days, doctors are not so lucky. They consult with their patients, give their advice and then hear what Dr Google has to say about that.

At the time of this visit to the doctor, Mum was 83 and was already on a lot of meds. Nine, to be exact, to treat her thyroid, diabetes, post-stroke issues, osteoarthritis, vascular disease, gout, depression and high blood pressure. And that was before the 'pams'. Clonazapam, diazepam (Valium), lorazepam and oxazepam all pop up in Mum's medical records going back years. She wouldn't have been the only woman in the '70s and '80s to have enjoyed the calming buzz of Valium, and she won't be the last. The pams are all benzodiazepines, which are basically calming medications used to treat anxiety, sleep disorders and panic attacks. Oxazepam, the one Mum was on in late 2016, was quite a hard-hitter, prescribed for anxiety.

It was true that Mum was getting more forgetful, but it was not true that Dad was getting fed up with her. Dad doesn't get fed up; he is the most patient person I know.

• • •

By the end of 2016 Mum was getting her medications muddled, which for someone with diabetes can be lethal. You have to take blood tests to measure your blood sugar levels, work out how much insulin to inject, then inject one sort at one time and another sort at another time. It was all very complicated.

Dad found her sitting on the bed one morning in tears.

'I can't do it anymore. I can't keep track of it all.'

That was when Dad took over her complicated drug regimen, creating a chart on the computer where he ticked off each medication and recorded blood sugar levels several times a day.

By the following April, Mum was starting to lose her short-term memory. She would forget where things were, forget things that had happened and, as is typical of people with dementia, she started leaving things on the stove and nearly burned the kitchen down. Twice. Dad took over the cooking.

By November the mood swings had arrived. Initially Dad just thought this was just Mum being Mum but doing it more often. The wonderful thing about my father is that he tends to soldier on and not get too caught up in the drama of life. If something bad is happening, he will just get on with it and block it out later. Problem solved. No residual bad stuff gets left in his head. There are whole periods of his life he can't really remember because they were stressful.

Typically, he never got Mum properly assessed for Alzheimer's or vascular dementia. These are very similar, but vascular dementia usually comes after a stroke, which Mum had had in 2012 during an overseas trip. She kept going with the trip and saw the doctor when she came home, who confirmed that she had probably had a small stroke. I spent hours wading through her medical records looking for a specialist's letter detailing Mum's dementia status, then finally gave up and asked Dad where it was.

'Oh, we never did that. The doctor told us she had Alzheimer's so we just accepted it.'

The records mentioned a referral to a psycho-geriatrician, but the appointment seems to never have happened.

My parents also made the decision not to tell anyone except my brother and me. Mum was terrified of people finding out and was deeply ashamed. She prided herself on being the most intelligent person in the room, and would often tell me in a rather Trumpian manner how terrific her brain was. She never quite used the words 'very stable genius', but came pretty close. She kept all of her high-school reports because they were evidence of great intelligence, with her coming top of the class most of the time. In pencil in the top right-hand corner she had calculated her average mark for each report — ranging from 61 per cent to 81 per cent. The comments were always very complimentary, describing her as 'bright and helpful', 'helpful and reliable', and congratulating her on her high position in the class, which was often first for the form. She was also appreciated for her help in the Stationery Department and her conduct was always 'very good'.

This is all fairly impressive when you think about what was going on at home for Elsie. Somehow she managed to overcome the dreaded biscuit jar, Mary's awful treatment of her, a strict and hypocritical father and a loving but chain-smoking and tantrum-throwing mother, plus five other siblings competing for attention.

Sadly, the subjects Elsie was allowed to study were designed for her future career as a typist. No Latin, French or history for my mum. Instead, the bulk of her studies came under the title of Commercial Work. She got top marks in book-keeping, shorthand, typing and commerce.

There was never anything Elis didn't know. She prided herself on being well read and kept up with all the latest politics — and made sure you knew it. Now, as she succumbed to dementia, she was going to try to keep that up and put on a show.

• • •

I could see that Dad was struggling to cope. Another sign of dementia in Mum was frequent falls, and the last one resulted in her breaking her ribs. Dad was unable to lift her and had to call an ambulance. Eventually he asked if he could take Paul and me up on an offer we had made years ago when we bought our house in the Hokianga. It has a two-bedroom self-contained unit (we call it a guest cottage) attached to the other side of our double garage. When Paul and I looked at the house before buying it, I said to Paul, 'That will be good for the parents.'

He nodded, but I don't think he thought it would ever actually happen.

Mum and Dad would often come and stay in the cottage and we enjoyed having them. They both loved the view of the harbour, and for Dad it was a dream come true. He had always wanted to live somewhere rural and by the sea. For a while they had a house in Mahurangi, but Mum would never live there full-time. She liked the city, the dinner parties and the bridge games.

But now it seemed that Dad might have his wish. He asked if they could come and live there permanently. He would sell their house and they would move in. We agreed immediately. We knew that this would take away our ability to have friends to stay — that cottage was a great guest house — and put some extra pressure on Paul and me to be on call for two ageing people. But in our minds, it was just what you do. You care for your old people for as long as you can. This was a perfect solution for giving Dad support to care for Mum but also leaving them with their independence, cooking their own meals and having their own residence.

The house sale was a nightmare, with Dad refusing any help to pack up or clean out or get advice on the sale price. There is something so stubborn and proud about Kiwi men in their eighties. They seem to think it is a weakness to ask for help. In the end I gave up and left him to it, thinking that I would deal with the fall-out after the fact, and it was, after all, his money to lose.

Shortly after the house sale went through, Mum and Dad came up to their new home to spend a few weeks relaxing after the stress of the sale before moving in full-time in January. We were still living mainly in Auckland at the time.

Dad rang me from the car after they had only been there a few days. They were on their way back to Auckland because Mum had gone dark. Really dark. She had accused Dad of tricking her into signing the house sale documents, and wanted him to ring the lawyer and cancel the sale. Then she would come right, and be horrified that she had been so nasty. Then it was back again to the new, dark personality attacking Dad constantly. Bad Elis was something he could cope with, but this was a new, improved and really scary version and he could not find a way to deal with her.

He decided that the only thing to do was bundle her in the car, take her back to Auckland and see the GP for some help in understanding this new condition. Mum was prescribed more pams. That was it.

• • •

The next few months were not easy either, as Dad packed up the house they had lived in for 30 years, grudgingly accepting some physical help from my brother. Dad arranged the removal trucks and made plans to head north.

That day I was in Auckland doing my daily afternoon radio show, so Paul met the house-moving truck when it arrived in the Hokianga and arranged everything in the cottage so that when they arrived it would look familiar for Mum. It looked terrific, as Paul has a talent for making things look great in a house, but it wasn't great for Mum. She continued to rage against Dad for selling the house for months.

'We own nothing! Nothing!' she would say.

I would try to interject and explain that they had the cottage they were living in. Paul and I had given it to them, and they owned it for as long as they needed it. And they had quite a lot of money in the bank, too, money they could spend on nice wine and treats.

'We own nothing!' she would exclaim.

At best, Mum thought she was having a nice holiday at our house and would ask me when they were going home. 'It's been so lovely having our little holiday here, you must kick us out when you've had enough,' she would say.

At worst, she was upset, distraught and discombobulated.

Dad and I realised that the dementia had progressed far enough for a change in environment to seriously freak her out. People with dementia hate change; they need everything to be in the same place and to have a set routine. Moving into the cottage completely unsettled Mum. Dad couldn't leave her on her own, or she would fret; so he would wait until we were there before leaving the cottage for more than ten minutes.

Eventually they got into a routine which involved Dad doing all the cooking, cleaning, caring and wine pouring while Mum's world reduced to sitting inside most of the day looking at the Hokianga harbour, which she seemed to enjoy.

Mum hated Dad doing the cooking and would daily remind me that he wouldn't *let* her cook. Sometimes if we were over there for a wine, she would get up and sidle over to the cupboards and the fridge. There would be a lot of opening and shutting of things for about ten minutes while Dad looked on nervously, and then she would triumphantly bring over a plate on which she had assembled 'nibbles' — 'zombie nibbles', as Paul called them. These foods were not your typical nibble foods. A whole can of creamed corn emptied onto a plate, some chocolate biscuits, slices of pickled beetroot, and to top it all off a couple of raw mushrooms. We pretended to have a nibble and left it at that. Dad would feed the whole lot to the chickens when she wasn't looking.

It was actually nice having them living up north permanently and keeping an eye on the place. Dad liked to feed the hens, do odd jobs and mow the lawns for us, which was great. They also loved our two dogs Rosie and Flo, with Mum deciding before too long that they were her dogs.

• • •

Dad says that despite the mood swings, those few years were his happiest with Mum. I think he liked having control over their life for the first time and not being told what to do by Mum. I think he also liked caring for her; plus, she was a brave patient. She never once complained about her condition, just felt sad and accepted it for what it was.

However, when she got on the wines at 4 p.m. with Dad things could turn nasty. I would often hear heated conversations between them as Mum was deaf and Dad had to shout so that she could hear him. It was always about Dad selling the house, how they owned nothing, and how he had tricked her. Dad knew that this was the dementia talking, but it didn't make it any easier to take. I'm embarrassed to say that when I witnessed it starting up I would leave them to it. Sometimes Mum would catch herself and then apologise profusely to Dad, finishing with, 'I guess you're just going to have to put up with me.'

I knew that once Mum had been served dinner she would be asleep by 7 p.m. and Dad would have the rest of the night watching TV by himself, which must have been bliss.

She was also still having the panic attacks that had plagued her all her life. She was very keen that she and Dad continue to visit their caravan in the Bay of Plenty. They both loved it there, and had spent many years snuggled up in their cosy caravan by the beach. Dad would pack the car and get everything ready to go, and then find that just when he was putting the chilly bin in the boot Mum would not want to go. So he would unpack and wait. This was quite the job, as Mum would insist on packing everything but the kitchen sink. Enough clothes to last a year, a sewing machine in case she felt like sewing, about 30 books and far too much food.

Then they would do it all over again the next day: Dad packing the car, Mum refusing to go.

Finally I suggested that he pack everything the day before, and in the morning just get her up, give her breakfast and pop her in the car, saying they were going for a drive — before she had a chance to panic. That worked, for a while.

CHAPTER 14

Demented Mum
and me

For me, demented Mum was an absolute delight. Having been terrorised by her for most of my life, to the stage where I couldn't hug her anymore without feeling nauseous, Elis turned into a sweet little girl. She was childlike in her mannerisms, really loved being visited and developed a sing-song-y way of talking. She would ask what day it was and be so surprised! Then five minutes later she would ask again and be so surprised again.

She would take great delight in receiving things, like a new cookbook. She would spend hours going through cookbooks putting little slips of paper in to mark recipes she would never cook. But she didn't know that.

I've kept some of them as a memento. Annabel Langbein had always been one of Mum's favourite cooks. We would often turn up for a meal in the old days and be told that it was 'one of

Annabel's'. In Annabel's latest cookbook, Mum had torn strips from a magazine and used them to mark 'smoked salmon pâté', 'Mexican shrimp cocktail', 'Pacifica chicken bites', 'chicken liver salad with hazelnuts', 'Thai style beef salad', 'Wanaka cheese scones' and 'miracle mayo'. All resonant of a '70s dinner-party menu. Over in Jamie Oliver's cookbook she had marked 'quick sausage meatballs', 'baked cauliflower', 'potato salad with smoked salmon', 'Welsh rarebit with attitude' and 'winter vege coleslaw'. It seemed that in the world dementia had granted her, food still brought her tremendous enjoyment. In these books it always looked delicious, and she could read the ingredients and imagine herself cooking it. When I visited op shops I would grab any old *Cuisine* magazines I could find along with any cookbooks from her heyday in the '70s. She loved them, and they would give her hours of entertainment.

• • •

Some days Mum was very aware of what was happening to her, and others not at all, in fact away with the fairies. There would be another person in the room quite a lot; visitors we were never aware of. She would quite often look at them but not include them in conversations. Later she would say, 'Did you see that woman sitting over there before?'

I would say, 'Of course, she seemed very nice.'

She also lived in the past and would tell me long, often funny, sometimes harrowing stories of her childhood. Including the biscuit jar.

For some people, talking to a person who repeats themselves and forgets things can be frustrating. In care homes I've seen some terrible examples of relatives constantly correcting their demented person. 'No that's not right, no that didn't happen. Honestly, I just told you that five minutes ago!' The key to spending time and talking with someone with dementia is to just go with the flow, and get used to repeating yourself without rolling your eyes or using a frustrated tone of voice. They're not deliberately trying to annoy you; they can't help it. It does take a bit of practice, but eventually you get really good at coming up with several different responses to the same statement. My mother-in-law Valmai also has dementia, and will often tell me twenty times in twenty minutes about her sore back. I pride myself on having a different answer each time. 'You need a couple of Panadol for that,' I'll say. 'You must have slept funny,' or 'Let's put a hotty on it.' Once you get into that it can be quite fun.

Mum was relatively easy to care for during those two years when she lived with us. When she wasn't childlike and full of wonder, she was having fun in the clouds or with imaginary people. Mum and I would go on fantasy journeys together, during which I would learn quite a lot about my mother that I'd never known. I was also quite safe from Bad Elis and Lady Elis, who seemed to have been murdered by dementia. Thank you, dementia.

During this light and airy, sunny time in our relationship, I often imagined with a thrill exactly how Mum's demented brain was starving Bad Elis and Lady Elis of oxygen until they shrivelled up into nothing. I had lived in fear of those two Elises all my life; now they were gone. I couldn't believe my luck. Finally I was getting the mother I had wanted all my life. Cheery, loving, sunshiny and pleasant to be with. Dementia had saved my relationship with my mother and bought me some time to find out what it is like to have a mother who is constantly in the same personality (albeit demented).

I knew we were very lucky. There are many stories of perfectly lovely old people turning into horrible, abusive and violent people in the throes of dementia. I saw it a lot in care homes later on. One woman in particular haunts me to this day. She would sit in the day room with a large teddy bear and systematically beat it to death. Really violently, like she knew what she was doing. When she wasn't beating up the teddy, she was yelling abuse at her neighbours and the staff. If a staff member came too close, she would lash out and hit them. Imagine how terrifying and distressing this would be for her family.

Instead we had Nice Elis, who was quite happy as long as she had a cookbook to look at, a comfy couch to doze off on in the sun, and plenty of food. She was also not a wanderer, which can often be a problem. She had lost most of her movement and could really only walk two metres at a time.

I started playing Scrabble with her because she was a wicked player in her time. You never won a game with her.

'We shall play at 11 a.m. every day, just let me know if you can't make it,' she told me, issuing instructions as only a mother can do to her daughter. My dad gave me one of the many long looks he gave me across the room which said 'you don't have to'.

I accepted. I had given up my broadcasting job in the city to do just this. To give Dad some time off to potter around our two-hectare property and work on carpentry projects, which he loves nearly as much as online shopping. As Mum's full-time caregiver he could never leave her for long, as she would become confused and upset if she couldn't see him. Scrabble gave him some respite.

So Mum and I began our daily Scrabble games. Sometimes I would stretch the rules a bit to let her have a word the Scrabble dictionary wouldn't allow. And occasionally I would deliberately leave a triple word score open for her to use. After a few weeks of this, I arrived for our game and Mum set it up enthusiastically. And then she looked me in the eye and proceeded to play the meanest game of Scrabble I had ever witnessed. She blocked me out, she refused to open up the board, she effortlessly placed Qs and Zs in long words, earning big scores that I totted up on my little pad.

'Oh my god, her brain has woken up,' I thought to myself as I pathetically placed the word 'dog' on the board.

And then she started helping me. 'If you had an "O" you could put it there and do very nicely,' she offered.

We finally finished the torturous game and I congratulated her on her efforts.

'Is it Wednesday?' she asked.

According to the notepad where I wrote down our scores, our first Scrabble game was on 12 February 2018. Mum won with a score of 232 to my 217. By the time we played our last Scrabble game in March 2019, her score was 186 and mine 251. I could have let her win, but by that stage she really didn't care who won. She just loved playing; and I would be lying if I said I didn't enjoy winning for the first time in my life.

• • •

Occasionally Mum and Dad would have visitors, but Mum really wasn't up to company. She would nod her head and contribute to the conversation with 'Oh is that right' and 'Well fancy that', but it was obvious to everyone that she wasn't keeping up. Her deafness and her refusal to wear hearing aids didn't help.

Occasionally she would insist on being taken out to dinner at the local Copthorne Hotel in Ōmāpere, but that ended one day when she looked at Dad across the table and simply said, 'I can't do this. Take me home.' The stimulation and change of scenery were too much.

After a while I noticed that Mum was wearing the same clothes for several days, and asked Dad how she was getting dressed. He pointed to a pile of clothes on the armchair by the bed and said she usually just rummaged in there. I waited until they had both gone away to the caravan, then investigated the bedroom. None of the dresser drawers had clothes in them. Instead, Mum had simply piled them all on the armchair or in bags lying around the room.

This was not something Dad seemed to want to get involved with, so I took the whole lot and washed what I could and threw out what I couldn't. Then I got three open cane baskets from The Warehouse and labelled them underwear, tops and pants. I sorted all the clothes into the three baskets, and when they got home I explained the system to Mum and Dad. It worked for a while, but then the clothes found their way back to the armchair. People with dementia forget what is in cupboards or drawers, so it is easier for them if clothes are out where they can see them. Some people take pictures of what is in a cupboard and then tape it to the outside of the door so that they can see what is behind the door.

Mum also stopped sleeping properly. She would wake six to eight times in the night, often confused about what time it was and where she was. She would wake Dad and he would settle her back into bed and talk her through it. One thing which was a tremendous help was a clock designed specifically for people with dementia, which has on its face not only the time of day but also whether it is morning, afternoon or evening and what day of the week it is. It has a dim screen so that it can be on in the bedroom all night and help settle distressed people.

Mum would quite often sleep most of the day, mainly because she lost so much sleep at night. She had always been a keen napper, sleeping in the afternoons most days, but this was more-constant napping, waking for short bursts then back to sleep. Dad would doze too, but the night-time sleep deprivation was taking a toll on him.

• • •

I know that Mum missed her social life in Auckland: her trips to the bridge club, having friends around for coffee, lunches and dinners. But the reality was that most of her friends were dead, and others had not kept in touch after Mum's dementia started to kick in and she couldn't play bridge anymore. Instead Dad would take her for drives, or I would. We would sometimes visit friends nearby for a game of Scrabble and lunch. Anything to get out of the house.

She would sit quietly in the front seat and be absolutely delighted at everything she saw.

When I was doing my radio show, a listener contacted me and told me that she cared for her dad who had dementia, and his daily drives to the seaside kept him going. 'Every day it was all new to him and he loved experiencing it all over again.' Mum was the same. She loved looking out across the paddocks and out to sea on our drives into Kaikohe. She would sit patiently in the car while I did my errands, then I would buy some lunch and we would drive to a park up on a hill and eat it looking out over the town. It was always the same for me, but not for her.

We would have lovely chats. In the confines of my small Toyota Corolla she could hear me very well despite her deafness, and so we talked. About her revolting childhood where food was a major theme. About her not having enough, and her sister having her own biscuit jar. About always being hungry.

'Consider the lilies of the field, how they grow. They toil not, neither do they spin,' Mum would say as we passed some lilies growing in a paddock.

'Where's that from, Mum?' I asked.

'The Bible. Probably something we did at church.'

She was remembering her childhood where she played the organ at church.

'Bloody church,' she mumbled.

We drove a little further, both marvelling at the beautiful sunny day, with light fluffy clouds in the sky — a perfect late winter's afternoon.

'Have you ever walked in the clouds, Wendyl?' she asked.

I took a moment and then answered. 'No, Mum. What is it like?'

'Oh it's a lot of fun, but getting from one cloud to another can be a bit difficult. Once you're there, it's very enjoyable.'

She stared at the clouds a little longer and then switched her attention to the paddocks again.

I didn't laugh. I didn't react. The last time I had had a conversation like that it had involved a lot of recreational drugs. Instead, I indulged in a moment's thought about what it must be like to think you can walk in the clouds. Not bad, I imagined.

Mum would forget things on a five-minute cycle. Sometimes she would come out with things that were in her imagination. She saw two cats when there was one. Mum used to hate cats because her sister with the biscuit jar once threw one at her. She has avoided them ever since; but now, in her new state, she quite liked them.

Mum's brain was busy exploring a new dimension, one she wasn't unhappy with and where all her needs were met.

• • •

I've seen people like my mother treated with pity and condescension — as if this 85-year-old woman is a child. My mother was not a child. She was a woman who had raised a family, taught children at school and had a past that can't be ignored. She had a good intellect and was a top-class bridge player.

During this time I read an amazing book called *Somebody I Used to Know*, written by Wendy Mitchell, who was diagnosed with early dementia at the age of 58. She has been very active in educating people on how to deal with a demented loved one, and she makes a very good point about dealing with the fantasy side of it all. She would quite often see her dead parents and have conversations with them.

Mum would quite often think she was still teaching, and say that tomorrow she was going to drive down to the local school and offer herself as a relief teacher. Dad's reaction would be swift and one of horror. 'Of course you're not, you can't teach anymore and you haven't driven in years.'

In Wendy's book she points out that there was no harm in her having a fantasy life for a while.

> *Did I think in that moment that Mum and Dad were*
> *still alive? Probably. Did it really matter? Probably not.*
> *I don't need to be told over and over that Mum and Dad are*
> *dead; what difference does my fantasy make to anyone else?*
> *People without memory problems often forget that those of us*
> *with dementia think about things in the past, and so the helpful*
> *response is probably to 'go along' with our experience, rather than*
> *trying to pull us back into the present day. It's not unethical to*
> *do that; it's just valuing the person's experience.*

I talked to Dad and suggested that he try to 'go along' with Mum's fantasy world. There was no harm in it.

Mum's physical health declined quite rapidly during this period. It was impossible to control her eating because she had no concept of what she had just eaten and, of course, her favourite soothing activity was to eat. She seemed to be eating most of the time, and nothing Dad could say would change that. When she got up in the night to go to the toilet she would stop off in the kitchen and fill her fists with biscuits, like a child, to be consumed in bed when she got back. At last she could eat all the biscuits she liked.

When we cleaned out her bedroom after her death I found biscuits, lollies and chocolates hidden everywhere, all in gift packaging. She had obviously told Dad that he needed to buy these for presents for people, then popped them away for snacks. I'm sure that in her dementia she had no idea where she had put them, but as they were in every drawer it wouldn't have taken much to find them.

One day I arrived for our Scrabble game and found her sticking a finger into the mustard jar and tasting it. She didn't know what it was. Another day I dropped off a jar of jam I had made, and returned ten minutes later to find she had eaten the whole thing with a teaspoon.

So she gained weight, which exacerbated all her other illnesses and made it almost impossible for her to walk further than a metre without wheezing and collapsing from the strain. Most months, Mum and Dad visited the Rawene Health Clinic about her various ailments. Then it all turned pear-shaped. I had done a lot of research on how dementia ends. Google 'what to expect in the last stages of Alzheimer's disease', and prepare yourself for some pretty sad news. Inability to communicate, inability to sit or walk, inability to control holding the head up or swallowing, inability to control bladder or bowel function, full-time daily assistance with bathing, dressing and eating. I knew that eventually Mum would have to go into care.

I tried to talk to Dad about it, but not only did he not want to know what would happen to her down the track, he also couldn't countenance the thought of her being in a care facility. I gave him the same books I was reading to work out what was happening to my mother, with pages marked for him to look at; he would return them to me the next day, having not looked at them. He was taking things one day at a time, and that was how it would be. There was nothing I could do to change his habit of a lifetime of avoiding tough stuff.

I knew that Dad was skating on thin ice and really only just managing to care for Mum with our support. He was 86 years old and in good health, but he was an old man who needed some support himself. Not that he realised this. He just kept going.

CHAPTER 15

Easter stroke

Paul and I were in Auckland in the lead-up to Easter 2019 because it was Paul's birthday on 17 April and we always like to get our large family together to celebrate it. I left Mum and Dad in reasonably good condition, although Dad's back was playing up. He was having a recurrence of a back condition he is prone to, which sometimes leaves him in so much pain that he can't move. But he seemed okay, so we hopped in the car and took off on Thursday.

On Good Friday I called Dad to check in on things. He was fine. Paul and I went for a nice long walk in the sunshine, and by the time I got home at about 1 p.m. it was not fine. Dad called to say he couldn't move. At all. Could I come back up?

I said I would leave immediately, and rang some friends who lived nearby in the Hokianga to go around and sit with Dad and Mum until I got there. I drove up reasonably quickly, but was only marginally concerned. Dad would need to rest and I would take over looking after Mum. Not a drama.

What I hadn't realised is that I would be getting there well into drinkies. Mum and Dad always started on the wines at 4 p.m., and my mother would be well into it by the time I got home. Nothing, and I mean nothing, stopped her from having her daily wines.

I drove down the driveway at about 5.30 p.m. I found Dad in his La-Z-Boy in his office, looking strained and clearly in pain, while Mum was sitting in the lounge with my friends, looking odd. I asked her how she was and she couldn't talk; she was slurring. This wasn't unusual when Mum had had a few, but to my trained eye something was a little bit different to the usual slurring.

'What's going on with Mum?' I asked my friend.

'She had three glasses of wine really quickly, and I think she's drunk,' he said.

Mum was really pleased to see me and was trying to tell me she liked my hair. I never usually wear my hair loose up north because it just gets in the way, but I had made a special effort for Paul's birthday dinner and it was still looking pretty fancy.

It was then I noticed that the left side of her face was drooping and her left eyelid was almost closed.

'I think she's having a stroke,' I said, quite loudly.

• • •

Everyone crowded around her and then I rushed next door to get the 'are you having a stroke' sticker off my fridge, which I have had there since Mum and Dad moved in for just such an occasion.

There were four things to do. Check for slurred speech, drooping side of the face, inability to raise arms in the air and call 111.

'I think we should call 911,' I said to my friends.

'111,' they said, correcting me.

'Fuck, I've been watching too many American crime shows!'

While my friend dialled 111, I tried to get Mum to lift her arms. It wasn't happening.

And then we waited. Where we live, ambulances might come from Rawene, which is fifteen minutes away, but more often they come from Kaikohe, which is 40 minutes away. In the end one arrived 90 minutes later, by which time Mum's face seemed to be better but she was still slurring. She just wanted to go to bed. I wouldn't let her. Dad had managed, very painfully, to get out of his La-Z-Boy and hobble into the lounge where he sat next to her on the couch and held her hand. He was completely freaked out.

When the ambulance finally arrived, her blood pressure and vitals were fine. I left Dad to my friends, who agreed to give him some dinner and stay the night because Paul wouldn't be able to get up until the following morning. Mum and I got in the ambulance and began a pretty bumpy journey to Whangārei Hospital, which took two hours. Mum lay in the ambulance in a fairly relaxed manner. I think the alcohol may have helped to subdue her somewhat. Her vitals remained normal all the way and I began to wonder if I had over-reacted.

We finally arrived at Accident and Emergency at Whangārei Hospital at about 9 p.m. and it was pretty quiet being Good Friday. There was the usual array of drunk, drugged people and some very sick and broken people. We had to stay there under observation until nearly 3 a.m. During that time, Mum was awake and a bit confused, but happy to follow instructions and read her book. She wasn't actually reading it, though, just looking at the pages. I think she had lost the ability to read a while ago and she mainly read cookbooks these days anyway.

The doctor appeared after a few hours, and he was your typical A & E doctor. Caring but brisk, busy but efficient, kind but practical. He was tall with grey hair, and I rather rudely wondered why an old guy like him was doing late-night A & E work. He told me that they suspected a small stroke or TIA (transient ischaemic attack), and that they would keep her in for the night and transfer her to the stroke ward. He said that the ideal thing to do would be to get her in and out of hospital quickly so that she didn't catch any bugs while she was in there. He ordered a CT scan and also a chest X-ray because she was wheezing. She had always wheezed, but it would alarm every health professional who met Mum.

The nurses were amazing, of course, and I would see for the first of many times how strong they were, lifting Mum on and off trolleys. Mum was pretty out of it the whole time but quite relaxed.

While we waited for test results I wandered the corridors, helping myself to instant coffee after instant coffee in the kitchen area. I read every poster on the wall advising people what to do if they felt unsafe, and gazed at Alison Mau's grumpy face telling me 'It's not OK to make your kids feel worthless, just because you're having a bad day.' I spent a moment or two wondering what kind of impact this privileged white woman had on the predominantly low-income Māori clientele using the hospital services that night.

There was a family there with a sick kid and three gorgeous kids in their pyjamas being really well behaved. I heard the nurse ask her superior if they could all bed down for the night because all the motels were full at Easter, and besides, she whispered, she doubted the mum could afford it. I heard the head nurse say it's not usually allowed, but it's okay. When I walked down the ward later they were all tucked down the end on mattresses, fast asleep, while their mother remained wide-eyed and focused on her sick child.

• • •

We were finally admitted to the stroke ward at about 3 a.m. It had three other people in it. I had a chair by Mum's bed, and she was so sweet, moving her feet so that I could put my feet up on the bed. Once again I so loved my new demented mother.

There was a man next to us who had also just been brought in. His name was Frank. We were to get to know Frank and his family really well over the coming months. Frank was 80, sporty and fit, and went to the gym a lot just so that this wouldn't happen to him. He was tall and big and kept trying to escape, which meant all hell breaking loose as his son attempted to contain him and ring the bell and get nurses to help.

We had a pretty rough night; my Fitbit showed no sleep. But I felt a little smug because Mum couldn't walk very far so was unlikely to try to escape like Frank. At 6 a.m. when she finally dozed off, I walked down the hall to get another instant coffee and ring Paul, who was in the car heading north to look after Dad. I was away for ten minutes and arrived back on the ward to find that Mum had got out of bed and had a fall. Because of her dementia she had forgotten she couldn't walk, I guess.

The head nurse, who was in as a relief worker for the Easter holiday, had a blind fit. I grew to learn that falls in the stroke unit were akin to drowning a baby. There was zero tolerance for it; staff had to fill out multiple forms and it was reported to higher authorities. From then on I had to alert a nurse if I was going to leave Mum to go to the toilet or grab a drink, and she soon had a watcher, someone whose job it is to sit and watch the stroke patient to make sure they didn't escape. Mum had one watching her every day and every night while she was in the stroke ward. The watchers were lovely people and often helped the busy nursing staff, too.

I stayed with Mum for the morning, then found a motel nearby and disappeared after lunch to grab a few hours' sleep. On my walk back to the hospital from the motel, one of the nurses who had been on duty when I left at lunchtime was driving home. She pulled over and told me that Mum had made several bids for freedom, so they had shifted her to a bed by the door in the ward where they could all keep an eye on her from the nurses' station.

I stayed with Mum while she had her dinner, then went back to the motel where I washed her clothes and got them in the drier, ordered a pizza and slept for twelve hours. This was the beginning of the 'will she, won't she?' existence that every family goes through with a stroke patient. Will she die tonight or won't she? Will I get a call in the night saying the big one has hit? I had googled Mum's condition and made a point of talking to any nurses who had time to listen to me, and was told that the likelihood of a person having another stroke after a TIA like Mum had had is very high. Basically we were all waiting to see if that happened.

• • •

On Sunday morning I was really hoping that we could bring her home, so I turned up as Mum was having her breakfast and waited for the doctor. He gave Mum a good going over and then said that he felt she was unlikely to have any more strokes, so it would be safe to get her home. She certainly looked fine, was talking fine and was very keen to get home. I rang Paul and he started the two-hour drive from the Hokianga to come and pick us up.

This had been a fright, but we would monitor Mum more closely now and I would have to do something about the wines.

Mum was able to walk with a walker and seemed really well. We stopped at the hospital pharmacy to get Dad his prescription for tramadol, which was the only thing keeping his back calm enough for him to move. It also turned him into a zombie. Paul had been looking after Dad since Saturday when he had taken him to the nearby Rawene Clinic to find some pain relief, as nothing was working. They put Dad on a bed and basically tried drugs on him until something worked; after two hours, they found that tramadol did. It also made Dad extremely drowsy, so Paul was cooking his meals and caring for him.

Leaving the hospital, we went to Pak'nSave to get Mum some incontinence pads and a few other things. To be honest, I should have realised that the fact I was having to buy incontinence pads was not a good sign. This plan was ridiculous. I was taking an incontinent, weak woman who could hardly walk home to live with her 86-year-old husband who was in extreme pain and could barely move or think. But I just figured we would work something out.

Then Paul noticed that something wasn't right.

'She's not making any sense,' he said. 'Listen to her.'

I pulled the car over and took a good look at Mum. She was mumbling and pointing at things out of the window, and then I saw her face. Drooping. Fuck.

We were still in Whangārei. We could have turned around and taken her back to hospital, but for some reason I thought she was just tired or something. In times of stress you believe what you want to believe. So we drove two hours home with Mum mumbling away to herself. By the time we got there she had lost the use of her legs. She had quietly had another stroke on the drive home. We got her inside, and then she needed to go to the toilet so I helped her with that and then got her to the couch.

Dad wouldn't come out of his office — he said he was in too much pain, and I think he really was. Paul and I looked at each other. We couldn't have her at home if she couldn't walk and Dad was stuffed.

'What are we going to do? I guess I could get her to bed, but in hospital they were hoisting her into the bathroom and using bedpans. We have neither,' I said to Paul. 'So what now?'

'I have no idea,' he replied.

It was one of those moments in a crisis when no answers present themselves. I was exhausted and couldn't think straight. Paul was in shock at the deterioration of Mum, who last time he'd seen her had been happily chatting away about clouds. I rang the Rawene Clinic, about fifteen minutes' drive away, to see whether I could get a commode, thinking at least she could get on that to toilet in the night, but as I was talking to the nurse and she was asking about Mum's symptoms, we both realised she needed hospital-level care.

'If you can get her in the car and drive her here, we can help get her out at this end,' she said reassuringly. 'We have a room she can have.'

Dad looked relieved.

We put Mum in the car and I drove to Rawene. I was met at the back door by a nurse who helped me get Mum into a wheelchair and into the hospital. I was so relieved to see his kind face and, as the doors shut behind us, so relieved to be in a place of professional healthcare. I had given myself a hell of a fright.

The doctor was very honest and said that Mum would probably be there for a while as their physiotherapist wouldn't be there until Thursday. Rawene Clinic serves the wider Hokianga area, but is really set up for accident and emergency plus regular GP care, not strokes. So if Mum showed improvement she could stay there, but if not she would be out of there and back to Whangārei stroke clinic fast.

She was admitted into a room that was lovely and cosy and special. I was so appreciative as I watched two nurses take over Mum's care, getting her to the toilet, giving her meals and pills. Mum had her own room with an en suite, a television and French doors on to a balcony. Wow.

I left her there to dash back home to have a shower, change clothes and get some things for her, like some flowers from the garden, pictures of the family and some nice blankets and pillows. I arrived back to find her quite happy, and I had a nice La-Z-Boy to sleep in. We settled in and turned on the television, and she was soon fast asleep. She needed to go to the toilet a couple of times in the night and we managed it together with the walker. That is something I am glad I will never have to do again — wiping your mum's bum is sobering. I gagged at one stage and had to take deep breaths on the balcony.

By this time I was done in. I had spent three stressful nights with Mum and I was operating on a high level of stress. I had rung my brother, who lives in Auckland, on the Friday and kept him informed. As I settled into Mum's room on that Sunday night, I decided it was time for him to help out. I hadn't talked to my brother for five years, so it was a bit awkward talking to him about this — but he was ready and willing to help. He came to Rawene to take over at midday on the Monday, and I was glad to leave him to it. Although it was a bit weird seeing him after all that time, he seemed very keen to help and full of the right energy.

The first thing he said to me was: 'I'm really sorry about the time I helped Mum put your head down the toilet and flush it.' Good to have that sorted.

I went home and focused on Dad, who was still bedridden and very foggy. Weirdly, he didn't seem too worried about Mum and nor did he want to go and see her. He was doped up but not in too much pain, which was helpful. I realised that his reaction to Mum's stroke was one of shock and an inability to do much about it. I was very much on my own as far as my mother's care went. But now with my brother as back-up.

Mark rang later in the afternoon to say that the doctor at Rawene had spoken to the consultant at the Whangārei stroke clinic and they wanted her back for a CT scan, so she was off in the ambulance back there. I didn't drive over to Rawene to wave her off. I left her in my brother's care and kept a close eye on Dad in the meantime.

CHAPTER 16

Dead or alive?

T he first thing I noticed about the stroke ward in Whangārei Hospital was the equipment. So much of it. Hoists for getting paralysed patients in and out of bed. Stroke chairs designed to keep the patient slightly upright but unable to fall out; they're shaped a bit like big pods into which the stroke patient is lowered. An upright trolley which allows the patient to stand upright, but they're strapped in so they look a bit like a non-moving robot that is wheeled about. Mattresses which are full of air so that the patients don't get bed sores; you hear the pump turning on and off to maintain just the right balance for comfort. Boots that are strapped around the feet and calves, which are pumped full of air and then deflated to keep the circulation going.

Then there's the usual array of monitors which beep and alarm and generally do a great job of keeping an eye on how the patient's doing.

• • •

In Mum's ward there were three other patients. One woman who never woke up herself, but was being fed by nurses who woke her up to do so. She was visited once a day by a patient relative, who sat next to her bed and held her hand despite not being recognised or acknowledged. After a week she was transferred to a room across the hall on her own where she slowly and silently died.

Then there was Frank, fit, tall and a bit muddled, who had come into the ward the same night we did. I grew to love him and his family a lot as we all went through the same stages of shock, anger and resignation. Getting through our weeks on the stroke ward without this family would have been a lot harder. They were kind, thoughtful, funny and inclusive.

The other bed was occupied by a young nurse, in her thirties, who worked in the hospital and wouldn't shut up. Constant chatter on her phone, to the other nurses, or to herself, all day and all night. She left after two days, thank god, to be replaced by a very handsome French man in his forties who would often make eye contact with me and roll his eyes. He was very fit. Both of these people belonged to the group of the frighteningly younger stroke victims who get a hell of a shock, are watched for a few days and then leave, having seen the state of things to come if they don't listen to their doctor.

The aim of the doctors and nurses on the stroke ward seemed to be to monitor their patients and keep a wary eye out for more strokes. Which is what happened with Mum. Despite constant scans and tests there was no conclusive evidence that Mum had had a stroke, but it was clear from her physical symptoms that she had. She was confused, and numb on one side.

No one on the stroke ward ever really maps out for you what is happening, because what are they going to say? 'Your mother will be here for a month, during that time she will have six more strokes and lose her power to walk, talk and swallow.'

They are not going to say that. Nor do they know that this will be the outcome. Some people rally, and recover enough to go home on some medication and a slower life. Others don't. Mum was one of those. Initially I was hopeful that Mum would just be there for a week to be monitored, then she would come right and we would get her 'back up on her feet' and home. And indeed while we were there several patients did just that.

But while Mum continued to have the mini strokes or TIAs, I had time to sit in her ward and reflect on how bloody lovely people can be in times of stress and sadness. Frank's family were there all the time, and within days we had become friends, joking with each other, hugging each other and crying with each other. This family who were strangers just days before had become my buddies in a crisis.

In the early days I found a Scrabble board in the family room and played with Mum. I figured that keeping those brain cells exercised was a good idea. She wasn't quite up to her usual standard but that was okay; at least we were putting words on the board. But when she put down the word 'quod', I rather patronisingly told her that it wasn't a word but I'd let her have it anyway, under the circumstances.

'It is,' she said. 'I know it is.'

Frank's wife Fay asked me what it was.

I told them and laughed at my mother. 'She's not thinking straight but that's okay.'

Then Fay came over with her iPad and showed me on her screen that 'quod' actually *was* a word according to the dictionary. It's another word for prison.

Oh how we laughed . . . the whole ward . . . at me.

I looked at my mum with her droopy face and her slurred speech, and reminded myself that she is one of the most intelligent people I know, and of course she could still play Scrabble, silly.

But then Mum started declining. There was a urinary tract infection and kidney problems. There were a number of mini-strokes. There was the fall when she had another stroke. There were her other medical problems to cope with, too: diabetes, dementia, deafness. Things were not going well. I started to think that she would die quite soon.

• • •

On arriving in the ward one day, I found one of the health assistants enthusiastically helping Mum on her walker do a round of the hospital floor. I watched in awe — this was definitely the most Mum had moved in years — but the health assistant was cheering her on and it was obvious that Mum had no choice. She collapsed on her bed, breathing heavily, and promptly fell asleep. An hour later she had another mini-stroke.

Finally, Mum had a massive stroke that none of us was there for, probably overnight on 1 May. She lost the use of her right side, needed spoon-feeding and had trouble swallowing, so her food had to be pureéd and her liquids had to be thickened. Her speech was unclear and we could only make out about ten per cent of what she was saying.

I no longer thought she might die; I hoped she would die. She would have hated being in this condition and staying alive.

My brother and I met at the hospital and sat down for a discussion about our mother. He felt strongly that Dad should come over and see her one last time. But Dad didn't want to come. Dad told me that he woke up from a nap and saw her smiling face, and also as she left in the ambulance two weeks previously she said in a deep, clear voice, 'Goodbye, Cedric.' He seemed to think that it was goodbye. I was mystified by it, but everyone deals with grief in their own way and I didn't want to pressure him.

The doctors said they would call it on Monday, wanting to see if she improved over the weekend. If she did, then it would be a hospital care situation. If not, then palliative care. I actually had to google 'palliative care' on my phone because I couldn't quite accept that it meant a gentle slide into death.

I sat by Mum's bed and couldn't stop crying for most of the day. Her decline was so obvious; she was just lying there looking confused and didn't recognise me. I leaned over her and said, 'Do you like my hair?' because she always used to tease me about not brushing it and keeping it up in a topknot at home. I had just washed it and it was out. She leaned over and stroked it for a long time, like a loving mum with her little girl. More tears.

A doctor had 'the conversation' with me. If she didn't get better by Monday, then they would stop feeding her and withdraw medication, including her insulin, until she died.

I then thought I'd better get hold of the power of attorney documents in preparation, thinking that it would be me who would make the final decision. Paul found them at home, and we found that Dad was in fact Mum's power of attorney. And there was no way Dad was coming over to Whangārei to make the decision to let Mum die.

I rang our lawyer. He suggested that a letter from Dad's doctor releasing him from the power of attorney duties would do it. Paul organised that, with Dad's permission. I then went to see the social worker at the hospital to find out exactly what they did need, and she told me that it wouldn't be my decision — it would be the doctors'.

'Really?' I said. 'But we hold the power of attorney, we have her living will — we know her wishes.'

'They will be guided by the family, of course,' she said, firmly.

So that was it. News to us. We all thought that by the end

of the week Mum would probably be on her way out. And I have to say that none of us was too sad about it. We didn't want her to live the way she was: paralysed, unable to talk, unable to take herself to the toilet, unable to walk, and struggling with late-stage dementia so that every five minutes she needed to be told all over again that she had had some strokes and this is why she was like this. She would be shocked and dismayed, dealing with the sadness all over again, every five minutes.

• • •

I stayed with Mum on the Friday and fed her lunch and dinner, which was depressing lumps of mush, but she seemed to enjoy them. I couldn't understand much of what she said, but she did ask once why she was sick.

I really appreciated the support of Frank's family. There were three of them in the ward at dinner time and we joked and laughed, and I loved that. It can be very lonely on your own caring for someone. I started bringing coffees in to the ward for Frank's family and the nursing staff.

On Saturday morning I arrived at the ward after breakfast to find a sleeping Mum. She had started having apnoea pauses, meaning that she stopped breathing briefly. Not a good sign. There was quite a bit of groaning, but not in a painful way. She would wake occasionally and smile at me, then go back to sleep.

I wondered if her end would come before Monday. A nurse came over and whispered confidentially that on her records was written 'palliative care for next week', so now I knew the plan. She was going to die.

Mum and I had been two weeks in the stroke ward, and I was feeling very vague and like I'd been in shock. I didn't resent this time at all, though, and was so glad that I was there.

While the doctor was with us, she said Mum needed to take more fluids, as her kidneys were failing. They had this thickened apple juice, so I asked Mum if she'd like a wine, and she gobbled it down very quickly, much to the amusement of the doctor. So apple juice became wine.

Sunday came, and what a shit day it was. I arrived on the ward to be told by a nurse that another consultant had examined Mum and the palliative care plan was off. They claimed that she was well enough to go into a care home and they would be conducting an assessment for that on Monday.

Now I got angry. I realised that if Mum had been diagnosed with cancer we would have had a clear plan for treatment, choices to be made, timelines given, end-of-life care discussed, and as a family we would know exactly what was what and how it would be. With dementia and stroke, there is no such plan. If a stroke doesn't kill you, well, then you're on your own. That is how I felt.

I had a mother who couldn't walk, was frozen down her right side, could not toilet herself, needed a hoist to get her in and out of bed, could not feed herself and could barely talk — and she didn't deserve to be allowed to die? A young doctor who had been looking after Mum all week popped in, and I told her my concerns. She told me that what was happening was that Mum was in an acute stroke ward and there had been a decision that she no longer needed acute care as the stroke had declared itself. So now it was time to move her. I agreed with this, of course, but the doctors still wouldn't be drawn on whether they would decide on palliative care or hospital care in a home.

Mum was awake and stubborn, irritated and restless, and frankly distressing. Her speech had returned enough for her to say that she wanted to go home every two minutes, and because of her dementia she didn't realise she had a catheter in so kept wanting to go to the toilet. I had to keep telling her that there was a machine in her bladder doing it for her and showed her the tube. She would be okay for a minute, then back to wanting to go to the toilet.

'Why am I here?'

She needed to be told that she had had a stroke.

'I want to get up and go home.'

Still more explaining. I managed to distract her by playing with some word tiles, making words into a crossword pattern. Then she'd had enough. And then she got shitty. Brushing my hand off her shoulder, she started pulling faces and the lizard eyes were back.

Thank god Paul had arrived over the weekend to support me, because I hit a wall. After a whole morning of Mum's behaviour

I found myself raising my voice for the first time and saying, 'Are you listening to me?!' This is exactly what she used to say to me when she lost it. She looked at me and shut up. How could I be so uncaring and impatient? She couldn't remember anything past a few minutes. I needed to sort myself out.

Mum had been awake all day and it was now 2 p.m. I looked at Paul and said I needed a break. So I booked a massage down the road and left him to it. I was away for two hours, and felt so much better. Meanwhile, Paul had managed to get Mum to sleep for half an hour and had worked out that if he said 'You've just been to the toilet' she would be quiet.

When I got back from my break, Mum was sitting in the state-of-the-art stroke chair. She was in the sun being fussed over by one of the health assistants, who had the wonderful ability to talk to someone making no sense and have a conversation, something I found quite common in healthcare workers working with the elderly. Apparently she asked Paul, 'Who is this Des she keeps talking about?' Paul didn't know, but of course it was Mum's older brother. I looked down at Mum in the sun, and once again she said, 'I want to go home. I need to go to the toilet' — or 'the toiley', as she had started saying like a child. Earlier she had told me that her name was Elsie Peterson and she lived at Princes Street — her maiden name and childhood address. She was living in her childhood.

Mum looked up at me and said, 'You go!' So I did. I kissed her and said I loved her and thought to myself, 'I think this is the last time I will see you alive.' On the way out I grabbed my knitting that I had been keeping in her bedside cabinet. I would not be back.

• • •

Paul and I went back to the Airbnb I had rented and talked about why I had hit the wall. I felt like I had been run over by a steamroller. We walked in the evening sun to feed some apples to the horses on the property, and fussed over an old cat who had found us.

The next morning we made a plan. It had been more than two weeks since Mum had been admitted and we both realised that I needed a break from the 'will she, won't she?' stress. I would let my brother Mark take over and handle the assessment on Monday. If there was a big meeting to discuss her future with the family I would come over for that, but the way the hospital seemed to be run they would just tell Mark what they had decided.

If they decided palliative care, then I would need to find her a care home or hospice super-quick. Apparently hospices only take someone if they are pretty much guaranteed to die in a few weeks. If they decided hospital care to keep her alive, then just the care home.

I arrived back home late on Sunday and it was so lovely to be back in the Hokianga. It's hard to describe what it is like to be constantly unsure of your mother's wellbeing. Will she die? Will she have another stroke? Will she remain this way for the rest of her life? Will the doctors allow her to die?

I felt jetlagged from not getting good sleep, and it was hard to concentrate on anything for long. A bit like having a new baby. I was constantly restless and found it hard to settle. The only thing that gave me joy was cuddling my animals and pottering around my garden — I can do those things endlessly. And walking on the beach; that is always good for my head.

I went for a walk on the beach and realised that I had done the best I could for Mum. Short of killing her myself. I had looked after her, tried to ease her through the horror of having dementia and being in hospital, and tried to get the message across to the doctors that this was not how she wanted to live.

• • •

On Monday morning, Mark rang to say that three doctors had told him it would be palliative care but not at the hospital. I needed to find somewhere Mum could die. And quickly.

Then Mark rang back a few hours later and said that a social worker had butted in and freaked him out by saying Mum *wouldn't* be palliative care. She would be hospital care — which basically meant living in a care home indefinitely in her state and not being allowed to die.

I got really upset about that, and realised why we need better euthanasia laws. We should have been able to choose to allow Mum to die, honouring her wishes, not having to be bound by some long-winded list of regulations that had to be adhered to so carefully by doctors.

My mother had her living will that she had written more than a decade ago, and she had told us over and over again that if she ever ended up what she termed 'a vegetable', to kill her and put her out of her misery. She was a supporter of euthanasia and fully expected us to do what she asked. We always agreed, never really thinking about how that might work. Would we smother her with a pillow? Feed her an overdose of pills? Push her off a cliff? Or course not, because that would be murder.

What followed was two more days of 'will she, won't she?'. Will she die of kidney failure? Will the doctors announce her palliative or won't they? Mark stayed with her at the hospital, but had to sit in the corridor because the minute Mum saw him she would be trying to get him to take her home. It got so bad that she was put on sedatives.

Finally Mum had her assessment. It was hospital care — living care — not dying. My brother emailed me after talking to the doctors:

Key points are:
Not palliative care as of today, because she can still wake and eat. But because she's still an eater, the doctors can't say she'll die.

They've knocked all her meds back to a minimum.

Importantly, they've also stopped supplementing fluids through the IV. So unless she starts drinking more, that side of things will deteriorate.

They may give her some more sedatives if her agitation gets worse.

So the plan is: if there is a place for her at a care home, then she can be transported as early as tomorrow or Thursday.

So that was that. We were powerless to help end Mum's life because she could wake on her own and eat. I would later find out there was more that we could have done, if only we had known.

• • •

Should I have got in the car and driven the two hours to Whangārei Hospital, demanded to see the doctors and stamped my feet and asked for a second opinion? Absolutely. Did I? No.

I don't know why, because usually I'm a pretty tough nut. I can only think that after three weeks of stress I just didn't have it in me. I let my brother, who was the elder after all, handle the end, and so he handled it.

CHAPTER 17

Care home search

It was difficult finding a care home for Mum. Rawene Health Clinic just fifteen minutes drive away had no vacancies, although they were building more facilities. I was told that there was a severe shortage in Northland for care home facilities, so if I found a vacancy I should grab it. Kaikohe was the next nearest, but there were no vacancies. Finally it was down to Dargaville, an hour-and-a-half drive away.

I took Dad's dinner over to his cottage and said we needed to have a chat. He was still really unwell from his back problems, on heavy painkillers, and was losing weight. He rarely left his chair and seemed to be in a state of permanent shock about Mum. I started to worry that he would 'turn his face to the wall' and give up. You hear stories of husbands and wives dying just months apart. Was this happening to Dad? Was I now facing the decline and death of both my parents? This outcome would have seriously pissed me off, because in my heart I wanted Dad to live at least ten years after Mum and really enjoy the freedom of just being himself in the kind of place he had always wanted to live. To have a decade of joy.

I sat down on the couch as he started to eat his dinner in his La-Z-Boy chair.

'Mum is being discharged from hospital and I need to find her a care home. But it won't be palliative care. She will be fed and medicated and kept alive. There is nothing we can do about that. I'm so sorry.'

He looked at me and stopped eating. Just the thought of it made him lose his appetite. Dad wouldn't eat a lot over the next few months and would lose quite a lot of weight, as well as strength. He told me to do what I thought best. I left him watching TV and then went back home and made an appointment to visit Dargaville.

Before I left the next morning to see the Dargaville care home, I popped over to see Dad and found him in bed, literally facing the wall. I pointed out that he was no better and that the drugs were just hiding the pain, that he wasn't moving any better nearly a week after seeing the doctor. He started moaning about not wanting to go back to the clinic because the doctor was useless and it would be too painful. I then suggested he see my osteopath in Ōmāpere. At least we should see if there was anything she could do to relieve the pain.

He agreed, then called me back as I was leaving and said,

'Last time I went to an orthodontist he was bloody useless.' He had muddled up orthodontist and osteopath, and I lost my temper then. I told him that he needed to adjust his attitude and think more positively about getting better. 'You can't just lie there feeling sorry for yourself while I'm losing sleep over what to do with Mum and you don't seem to give a shit. You need to start moving and make an effort or I'll put you in a home, too.'

I managed to get out of there before I started crying, and then I sat in my bedroom wracked with sobs. A release from the past three weeks' dramas, and about time. I was so shitty that I didn't even say goodbye to Dad and asked Paul to take him over his breakfast.

Paul forgot, and by the time he did get over there Dad had managed to get out of bed and make his own breakfast.

• • •

I drove down to Dargaville and found that the care home was really nice. Quite old, but comfortable, the staff were pleasant and Mum's room had a view on to a garden and got the morning sun. At that stage I really believed she would just be there for a few weeks and would slowly die. I signed her up and made plans to get her transported from Whangārei Hospital in a few days. I had no idea that the next month would be even worse than the previous three weeks in hospital.

Luckily, Dad got a lot better after two sessions with the osteopath and came off the Tramadol, so was more awake and talking sense. He seemed to have said goodbye to Mum in his head, though, and was still resisting visiting her.

Then he had to get a biopsy of a mole on his back at Rawene. We got there, and all went well except that he had forgotten they had also booked him into the physiotherapist for his back. We went in. Dad immediately started out on his long story about his historical back issues and I could see that the physio did not want to hear it.

'You're down here to see me for a groin strain,' he said, abruptly.

'Oh that went ages ago,' said Dad in a rather curt manner. 'What you need to look at is my back problem.'

Things were not going well. I could see that either Dad or the physiotherapist was going to lose his shit so I interrupted and explained that Mum was dying, and we had both had a very stressful few weeks so please bear with us. That did it. The physiotherapist changed tack, got a little more patient and ended up being really good for Dad. He was happy that Dad was seeing the osteopath as she was excellent, and persuaded Dad to stop using his stick to get around and swap it out for a walker, just at night, as a much more effective tool against falls.

On the drive back, Dad and I had a big talk about what it was like living without Elis, and he said he was still adjusting to having some time on his own after nearly 65 years. He said the past two years had been hard and that Mum would get into moods where she was sarcastic and critical and mean. He understood that this was because of her childhood and her dementia, but that didn't make it any easier. I told him it was okay to be relieved and to plan his new life, and painted a picture of what that could be like. Getting fit enough to go fishing, do some gardening, get back down to the caravan. A new normal.

I talked to him about his finances regarding Mum's care-home costs, as they wouldn't qualify for a subsidy. He needed to pay for it all. I wrote it all down for him, as he was still quite vague. Dad also started talking about visiting Mum at last, and shortly afterwards started cleaning out his cottage of some of Mum's things.

• • •

On 16 May, Paul and I packed up the stuff we thought Mum would need in her new home. As we were doing so, I saw Mum sitting in her chair, which was waiting to be put in the car, and waving at me. Weird.

We drove down to the home I'd found in Dargaville and started setting up her room. It was small, with a standard built-in cupboard/wardrobe, a basin and a window looking out on to a garden. Her bed was hospital-grade and there was a La-Z-Boy chair there, too.

I popped Mum's toiletries into the bedside cabinet and then

we set up a TV for her and hung some pictures on the wall. We added a shelving unit and put family photos there, along with some flowers, and then waited for her to arrive. It still wasn't great, so Paul went off in a bit of a panic and bought some weird fish sculptures to put on the wall.

Mum was completely disoriented after what must have been a confusing ambulance drive on her own. Ambulances do not have great shock absorbers, and when you're in the back of one, country roads are not your friend. She was exhausted and fell asleep pretty much as soon as she was put to bed. We sat with her for an hour and then left to get back to Dad up north.

There was a feeling of having drawn a line under this mess. Mum was getting 24-hour nursing care, she was safe and comfortable, and her quality of life was no longer at the mercy of hospital doctors who kept changing their minds. It was done. She would stay there until whatever happened, happened. To be honest I thought she would die within a few weeks. I was wrong about that.

I just had to deal with the guilt of not seeing Mum every day. If she was around the corner then I probably would have popped in to see her often, but being an hour-and-a-half drive away this simply wasn't possible.

• • •

Two days after Dad's physiotherapist visit Paul and I drove to Auckland, leaving Dad set up with dog and hen food. We stopped in Dargaville to check in on Mum, and found her settled, then agitated, then sleepy. My cousin, who is a physiotherapist, visited her that afternoon and sent me a text: 'I have no doubt she recognised me and during our conversation she seemed to make entirely appropriate replies. I would say that lasted 6 minutes, then she got a bit agitated about something and began perseverating. So our conversation ceased. Her dysarthria (problems with speech caused by the stroke) is severe but I felt she knew what she wanted to say, poor thing, and it came out all jumbled.'

When Mum was really bad in hospital and I was holding her hand and crying, Frank's wife Fay had come over and said to tell her to let go. 'Just let go, Elis,' she said. 'Fall away.' This is what she had done with her own mother in the late stages of dementia and, looking at the state of my mother, she felt it was a good idea.

I personally felt it was a bit early for all that, but then I wondered whether that's what I should have been doing all along. Trying to access a neural pathway in Mum's demented brain to say it's time to go, it's time to die. I decided that every time I saw her I would repeat the mantra, adding the words 'stop eating if you want to die'. Death by words. We'll see.

At the care home, I started what I came to think of as my 'hi, die, bye' sessions with my mother. I closed the door to her room and sat down next to her, holding her hand. I looked deep into her eyes and started talking to her about the need to let go. To stop eating. To just let herself leave life and die. I shut the door because I wasn't sure if what I was doing was entirely legal, and also it might be frowned upon by her carers, who might write in their notes: 'Daughter keeps telling her to die.'

The next time we visited Mum, a few days later, she was a bit clearer but very much following the pattern described by my cousin. After a while, Mum said, 'You can go now.' She didn't seem to want us around for long. I chatted to the nurses and they were really lovely. I saw what they were feeding her for lunch, which looked really nice even though it was all puréed and her liquids were still thickened to prevent her from choking.

During that visit I shut the door to her room and leaned down close to her ear so that she could hear me well as I did the 'hi, die, bye' speech. 'You always said you didn't want to be like this, so now it's time to tell yourself to go, to die. Stop eating and die if you want to. Let go if you want to.'

She nodded as if she understood. I did it the next visit and a few visits after that, but then I stopped because I don't think she actually did understand; and if she had, she could never stop eating anyway because she'd rather die than stop eating.

• • •

Finally, Dad felt ready to see her. He got his clothes out the night before and checked them with me. Then he picked her some flowers. He was very nervous, I think. I was shocked to see how his clothes hung on him. He still wasn't eating much and I worried that he, too, might have something wrong with him. We drove down, chatting all the way. Dad and I have always been good chatters and are quite happy in each other's company.

When he went in to see Mum in her room at the home, she was so delighted to see him. He was shocked and got a bit teary. I left the room as I felt they needed some privacy and I was a bit upset, and got back after a while to find Dad holding Mum's hand. He looked at me, totally confused, and said, 'But I can't understand a word she says.' He hadn't been with her as she'd slowly deteriorated over the past month, so had not developed any skills for communicating with her as she was now.

'Watch this,' I said. I leaned over Mum so that she could hear me, and said, 'Dad has come, he's your friend.'

And she said, very clearly: 'He's more than a friend.'

'Of course, he's your husband,' I replied.

Dad said she was squeezing his hand the whole time and managed to get him to understand that she would like him to stay the night with her. After that she went into her confused, agitated state, and tried to get out of the bed.

Dad looked like a ghost by the time we left, and barely had the energy to get around Countdown and have half a toasted sandwich before we drove home. He worked through what he had seen on the way home. Is she still there or not? Does she know where she is, or not? I told him that because of the dementia she seemed to have a five-minute recall, so I thought that while she had moments of clarity, I doubted that she knew where she was and that we were lucky she seemed so calm.

While Dad was in the supermarket I had checked my emails, and there was her DHB needs assessment, which made for sad reading. How could you keep this alive?

Issues: Post Stroke
  Cognitively impaired
  Blood sugars will need close monitoring due to low food intake
  Assistance needed to eat and drink
  Communication issues
  High falls risk
  Restless at night, sleeping intermittently while in hospital
  Dependent with all ADLs (activities of daily living)
  Unable to transfer, will need a Hoist transfer and 2 assist
  Poor sitting balance
  Double incontinence
  Will need skin integrity maintained
  Significantly fatigued
  At risk of pressure injuries, will need assistance to change position.
    OUTCOME: SPA VERY HIGH, HOSPITAL LEVEL OF CARE

I couldn't find out what SPA stood for but I really didn't need to. It was bad.

While we were still driving home, the care home rang. It was the RN (registered nurse), who said that the doctor had visited. They had decided on round-the-clock paracetamol because they thought Mum was in pain. No kidding.

And her blood sugar readings were down to 5.6; almost normal. After 40 years of type 2 diabetes Mum was free of it, due to a month of a hospital diabetic menu and her inability to snack and drink wine. Fuck.

Dad talked enthusiastically about visiting Mum once a week as soon as he could manage the drive. His grief was taking a huge physical toll of him. While he wasn't showing a lot of emotion, he had become frail and felt he couldn't do anything. I worried that this had become a bit of a mindset, and so gently encouraged him to do some more walking, and perhaps just drive the ten minutes down the road to the osteopath. Paul and I were still cooking his meals, and were happy to do that, but I hoped he would come right and get back to his normal self eventually.

• • •

Dad and I talk every day, usually in the morning and then in the evening when he has a glass of wine. We discussed a topic I had been playing over in my head for the past few days.

What if we had just left her?

Should I have left Mum to have her stroke? At the time she was having it, she was tired and wanted to go to bed. What if we had left her to do that and allowed the big stroke to happen? Would she have died? Would that have been better? Instead, she was poked and prodded, given anti-stroke medication and eventually had the stroke anyway, although possibly not as strong a stroke as it would have been otherwise. I thought we should have left her. Dad wasn't so sure.

CHAPTER 18

The problem with care

Mum's birthday on 9 June came and went with us visiting her and making as much of a fuss as she could understand. Her sixty-fifth wedding anniversary three days earlier had involved flowers and a visit from Dad.

Mum's first week in the care home had gone well, but after three weeks it was not good at all. She gradually became very agitated and angry and furious. On each of our visits she would start to cry and try to get out of bed because she wanted to go home. This freaked everyone out, but I would sit there and talk to her and explain what was going on, and eventually she would fall asleep.

Then things took a terrible turn.

First, she fell out of bed. I asked the care-home staff to put a rail up on her bed to stop this happening again. When I next visited, there was no rail but she had been turned around to face the wall. This meant that her paralysed right side was facing the outside of the bed, preventing her from being able to move to the edge of the bed and fall out. She was basically staring at a wall instead of her window. The next time I visited after that, they had pushed her La-Z-Boy chair up to form a barrier, but there was still no rail.

On one visit, she had pulled all her clothes off and had been left there naked. I could hear her cries as I came down the hall. On another, she had taken her nappies off. On yet another visit she was crying out, and I discovered that she had her foot stuck in her nappy at an awkward angle. I asked that she be put on a strong sedative to reduce her agitation and suffering, as I thought she was in late-stage Alzheimer's, judging by her symptoms, which were basically severe agitation. According to my consultations with Dr Google online, it was also possible that her stroke had hastened her dementia.

The problem with the care home was that their doctor was the local GP, who only visited once a week and had little experience of dealing with dementia. Every time I requested something, it took a week to happen while we waited for him to visit. Eventually he prescribed quetiapine, which is used to treat schizophrenia, bipolar disorder and major depressive disorder, and can often work for people with dementia. It had little effect. We then had to wait another week for the doctor to come back to the care home and assess her and then increase the dosage.

All this time we knew that Mum was thrashing and wailing

and crying out. We could hear her from the end of her corridor every time we visited.

• • •

It didn't help that during this time some relatives visited and gave me hell about it.

They emailed Dad to complain about her condition, but Dad wasn't answering emails at that stage. He was still unwell and grieving and contemplating the wall. So then I got a text from them telling me she needed a better mattress, and needed to be turned and several other pieces of advice.

I lost my shit and sent this back: 'She already has a special pressure mattress which pumps up and down. She is agitated because she has Alzheimer's and wants to come home, it is mental not physical. Today she started on some antipsychotics for that and is already less agitated. I have been trying to fix this all week. It's really helpful if visitors who pop in once a month trust me to be doing the best I can for her and also my Dad who I have full care of. Sorry for the rant.'

I think this is one of the most difficult things about having a parent in a care home. Bloody visitors who pop in for half an hour and then criticise her care, or the room, or the staff, or the clothes she was wearing (or not, with my mother, who liked to pull her top off). Even if it is well meant. It's one thing to visit, and quite another to be the full-time carer trying to do their best in what was a pretty horrible situation.

Another relative rang me to say: 'NO ONE HAS BEEN KEEPING ME IN THE LOOP!' Turns out he had been emailing Dad, who hadn't been replying to him. So I had to talk him down and also encourage him not to visit Dad, who had no desire to see anyone. I felt so alone in this; my brother had removed himself from the situation now that the emergency was over, and Dad just handed everything over to me.

• • •

By now I was starting to feel some resistance from the care home about sedating Mum. I know there is a big push against sedating old people in care homes just to make it easier for the carers to look after them, and rightly so. But in Mum's case the sedation wasn't needed to make the carers' job easier, but to save Mum from her appalling quality of life. This was a woman who was paralysed on one side, could not talk, could not feed herself, was in nappies and incontinent and had dementia. Of course she was fucking pissed off. She had also been quite happy to sedate herself for most of her life on Valium and alcohol, so I figured she wouldn't have a problem with sedation now.

Despite the increase in the quetiapine dosage, Mum ended up being in a constant state of distress for three weeks. Finally, in desperation, I called the clinical manager to express my frustration. He was new and I hadn't dealt with him before. I was grateful that he cut to the chase and said that the care home was not a dementia hospital, and offered to call in a psychiatrist to assess Mum. Another wait while she thrashed and wailed. I told him that we were worried she was going to be kicked out of the care home because she was becoming too difficult, and he said that it was more a case of her needing more specialist care than was available there. A week went by and there was no call about the psychiatrist, so I rang and asked the clinical manager to follow that up.

Then one morning I woke up and had a moment of complete clarity. I realised with absolute certainty that I needed to get Mum out of there, and fast. Something with the care home didn't feel right, and reading between the lines I knew that they were not equipped to cope with Mum. I started looking for a dementia care unit straight away that morning. I did not want Mum to be in this state any longer.

Again I was faced with no vacancies anywhere, except one care home I hadn't been able to get Mum into at the beginning of all this. It was the Jane Mander Retirement Village in Whangārei, which had a dementia care unit. I knew that Frank — from Mum's stroke ward at the hospital — had gone there temporarily and his wife Fay lived in the village. I asked her what she thought and she said it was excellent, and she would put a good word in for us.

I went to see it, and holy shit it was like a hotel. You walk into this very grand entrance and all the furnishings and design look like a grand hotel or a luxury cruise ship. I'm sure this is very deliberate and I knew that if Mum was herself she would think this place was very nice indeed. That helped somehow.

I could see other people in Mum's state there, and immediately thought that even if Dargaville got Mum settled with medication I was going to shift her anyway. Dad agreed even though he hadn't seen Jane Mander. He trusted my instincts.

• • •

We had a meeting at Dargaville on 19 June for a resident review, during which they basically said that they hadn't been able to settle Mum but had requested a psychiatrist to visit. This was, I think, because they sensed that the local GP wasn't up to it.

I asked them if they felt that their place was the right place for Mum and if they felt capable of caring for her; and while I have to say they never said no, I could see that they were struggling. They did say that they weren't a dementia hospital. When I talked of our wish for Mum to be sedated, the nurse said: 'But that is a chemical restraint.'

It turned out that the care home had a 'no restraints' policy. This was why no bed rail had been put up on Mum's bed and why they were not giving her a lot of sedatives. This totally derailed me. No one had had a discussion with me about restraints, and had they mentioned they had such a policy I would have assumed this meant not tying people to beds, which of course I do not support. But I had never heard the term 'chemical restraint' and could not get my head around it. Sedating a woman so that she is comfortable in her own body, which is restrained because of a stroke, seemed like something you would do out of kindness, if nothing else.

Fortunately, the day before Jane Mander had called and said they could take Mum and could admit her on the Friday, two days away. So I told the care home that I was transferring her because I needed her to receive the care she needed, which obviously wasn't possible under a 'no restraints' policy.

Dad and I went back to Mum's room, where I noticed, once again, no rail on the side of the bed to stop her rolling out; three weeks after I had asked for one.

Then all hell broke loose. The nurses were all crying in the nurses' station and the manager, whom I hadn't seen since my initial interview, called me into her office. She said that we would have to pay a three-week notice period. I explained that the only reason I was moving Mum was that I had been told her facility couldn't care for my mother's condition and I no longer wanted her in a constant stage of agitation, which she had been in since 7 June, and at risk of falling out of bed. Keeping her there for another three weeks would be cruel.

The manager didn't like that. Later, after some emails back and forth, she withdrew the need for the three-week notice period.

In the end we arranged for Mum to be transferred to Jane Mander on the Saturday. I turned up at 8 a.m., which was when the ambulance had been booked for, and found Mum sleeping. I had asked the care home to give her a sedative to cover the ride. The ambulance didn't turn up so I asked for the number to ring. They gave me the number that was written on the wall in the nurses' station, and it was wrong. Christ.

The nurses who worked with Mum in the care home were all amazing. It takes a certain person to be so calm and caring and lovely. They were very physical with Mum, kissing her and hugging her, and you could see that Mum loved them back. Despite her obvious agitation she had become a favourite with the staff, and my dad and I will always be so grateful for the care they gave her.

While we waited for the ambulance, several nurses stopped by to say goodbye to Mum — they genuinely loved her and I could see that they had all been doing a beautiful job with her. A couple of them also told me that I was doing the right thing for her, which made me feel better. No sign of the manager.

The ambulance arrived, and I asked the nurses to change her nappies and give her more sedation, which they did. Then they handed over all her medication to me, including the little bottle of blue liquid containing her sedative. I knew this because I had seen them administer a few drops to her mouth beforehand and asked what it was.

As we waited, I looked at this little bottle of blue liquid for a long time. I considered dosing Mum with the whole thing. Would she die, or would she just have a big long sleep? If she did die, would I be caught? Of course. I opted instead to shut the door and top her up with a few more drops as the ambulance pulled into the driveway.

• • •

The ride along the winding roads to Whangārei was awful. Mum was really agitated, trying to get out of the seatbelts holding her on the stretcher and groaning. We got to the new home and received a lovely welcome. She nodded off.

Dad met me there. We had a good interview with the manager and clearly stated our thoughts on sedation, and then Mum was put in her room — where she lost her shit. She was screaming and trying to get out of the bed. It was awful. People with dementia hate change, and all Mum could see was that Dad and I were there but she wasn't home. Something wasn't right.

Eventually the doctor came to see Mum. After my last experience, I wasn't leaving until I had seen him. I needed him to know exactly what Mum needed. But I didn't have to go there. He took one look at her and immediately changed her medication and care plan, then and there.

He often paused as he was going through her medication and said, 'Why is she on this?' I said I had no idea. It was obvious that he had extensive experience with dementia patients, and assured me that there would be a rail on her bed within the hour to stop her rolling out and that she would be given enough sedatives to make a difference to her state.

Dad was starting to look like he would faint, so I told the nurses we couldn't stay to stop her getting out of bed in the meantime. They put Mum in one of the amazing capsule stroke chairs they had used at the hospital, and kept her in the nurses' station. I was impressed with their ingenuity. However, Dad and I left feeling like shit because the plan to get her more settled had left her much less settled.

I rang Jane Mander the next morning, and they said that Mum had settled and was pretty good. Paul and I visited that afternoon, and I was so relieved that for the first time in weeks she was very comfortable. We even got a few smiles. The nurses said that Mum had been quite tired after her journey, but had managed a few sips of champagne and had a foot massage at happy hour the night before. They also picked up that her right arm, which is paralysed, seemed to be giving her some pain so they had increased her pain relief. I wondered how long that had been the case.

We were so pleased to have found a home which specialised in Mum's condition and would also get her out of bed and into some activities, even if she couldn't really participate in them. I think she got very bored locked inside her head. I was also impressed with her room, which had French doors looking out on to a courtyard, her own hoist, her own toilet and her own special chair. It was amazing.

• • •

Mum's time at Jane Mander was the best we could hope for. Sometimes we would visit and she would be agitated, and so they would put her in the stroke chair in the nurses' station with them for company. Other times she seemed quite comfortable, if a little stoned. Which is what she would have wanted.

I felt confident enough with her care that I left for a long-planned two-week holiday in New York. The book I had been writing had been put on hold for two months while I sorted Mum out, so I figured I could do some writing over there as well as have a much-needed break. Dad was also improving and, while still frail, he was able to take care of himself.

While I was in New York I got a call from Jane Mander to say that Mum's blood sugar had dropped and she was unresponsive. So they revived her and gave her insulin. I called Dad and said, 'What the fuck? I thought we said do not resuscitate?' I fired off an email to Jane Mander to ask for clarification, and got this explanation in reply:

> *For Elis — the checking of her blood sugar levels, administration of insulin and provision of glucose when blood sugar is low, is as*

important to her wellbeing as say eating or drinking. Diabetes is a long-standing condition and as such we monitor and provide insulin or glucose as part of our basic duty of care and would not be appropriate as part of our duty of care to withhold.

So insulin was like food. Legally they had to give it to her.

I arrived back in Auckland and drove up to see Mum. She was in the lounge and was a little more droopy than usual; her head was lolling more. She recognised me and we sat together. She held my hand and examined my wedding rings closely, then my watch, then touched my hair and stroked my arm. I told her about New York and she seemed to understand because she kept saying 'oh' in a surprised fashion. The carer told me that Mum was having good days when she would be alert and then would basically sleep for two days to recover. I had got her on a good day. She dozed off for a minute, then woke up and said very clearly, 'I would like a cigarette.' I laughed and said, 'Wow, you haven't smoked for years. Shall I pop out and get you a packet of Pall Mall Menthols?' — which is what she used to smoke. She laughed at that, had a good chuckle. She then started to doze off again, so I kissed her goodbye and left.

That was the last time I saw Mum alive.

CHAPTER 19

Dying lessons

'S he died in her sleep. It was so peaceful.'

It's a nice thought, isn't it? To die in your sleep. One night you go to bed with your glass of water on the bedside table, read a few pages of your book and then turn out the light, snuggle under the duvet and get into your favourite position. You drift off, totally unaware that in a few short hours you will be dead.

This death is very unlikely to happen to you. In this country, according to the latest statistics available, most people die of cancer and heart disease. Neither of those deaths is particularly pain-free or peaceful. In the UK the leading cause of death is heart disease, but the second leading cause of death is now dementia and Alzheimer's disease, something that is predicted to also happen here as we live longer and dementia becomes the norm in old age.

The number of New Zealanders living with dementia is growing rapidly, according to Dementia New Zealand. It is estimated that in 2020 there are around 70,000 New Zealanders living with dementia. This is expected to rise to 102,000 by 2030, and by 2050 the number of people living with dementia is expected to have almost tripled to 170,000.

One of the biggest problems we have in identifying the numbers of people affected by dementia is that when they die, doctors are more likely to put 'pneumonia' than 'dementia' on the death certificate. This means that the dementia isn't counted. My mother's death certificate says she died of pneumonia, cerebral thrombosis (blood clot) and diabetes. So despite being cared for by her family for several years of dementia, she is not counted as a sufferer.

Many of us are watching our parents die, and it's awful. We mutter the phrase 'I wouldn't let my dog suffer like that', and then we sit and watch and visit and hold hands and wait until their agony is over. Then we start to think about how we can prepare ourselves for this sort of death — or perhaps avoid it completely, which is my preference. None of us wants to die the way our parents are dying, let alone spend the final years of our lives in a care home. Yet hundreds of people around the country are getting placed into care homes every day when they would rather be dead. You might think that there is not a lot you can do until decent euthanasia laws are passed, but as I was finishing writing this book I found that there is some stuff you can do in advance.

I had bought a book called *O, let me not get Alzheimer's Sweet Heaven!* by Colin Brewer. For a start it had the worst book title in the world, and when it arrived in the mail I looked at the garish red artwork on the cover and wrote it off as some self-published nightmare, and put it on the book shelf, leaving it untouched for a few months. But a review in *The Times* newspaper had said that this book would give you the tools to ensure that you died the way you wanted to. I think I had possibly had enough of dementia and dying at the time to bother reading it when it arrived.

When I reached this chapter in my writing process, I got it off the shelf and read it. I then spent two days steaming with anger and rage.

• • •

Here in this book was everything you needed to know about advance directives, why it is important to have one and how they are legally binding. I realised that if I had got Mum to do one she would have been allowed to die peacefully in a diabetic coma. She would not have had to spend ten weeks in a care home half alive and constantly fretting, costing my dad $1000 a week of his savings and leaving us feeling inadequate and uncaring in the process.

I write this as a warning to families. Everything about the hospital environment encourages families to 'go with the flow', to respect the medical decisions made for their loved one because only the doctors know how to save their lives. But does this mean that only the doctors have the right to decide when a person should die — or not, in my mother's case? Absolutely not, and I totally dispute their supposed power to do so.

When a woman is about to give birth, she is prepped about everything that will happen before, during and after the birth. She is factored in on every decision, warned of every danger she and her child might face, and protected and encouraged and included. Death in this country does not have the same privilege. It is still clouded in some sort of Victorian shadow where the doctors decide when, how and why a person will die.

I think that every family who has a family member in some sort of critical condition should be counselled about their rights, listened to by the doctors and encouraged to share their wishes, on behalf of the critically ill person. Instead we must resort to other means, such as organising an advance directive which in our case we had known nothing about at the critical time.

I also wonder whether the fact that dementia is an illness which has no cure is a factor. There is no money to be made out of dementia patients in the form of expensive pharmaceuticals. I'm being very cynical here, but if you are diagnosed with cancer or heart disease, plans are made. You are given treatment options, drugs, surgery and a plan, even if that plan includes the fact that you only have twelve months to live. People make a lot of money off you. With dementia, you are diagnosed and then sent off with this progressive disease to decline slowly and be in the care primarily of your family or friends. In New Zealand, 70 per cent of people with dementia are cared for at home, with family members providing the majority of the care 24/7. There is also no support plan for someone diagnosed with dementia, which is shocking considering that the average life expectancy for someone with dementia is ten to twelve years. That's a long time to live without a plan.

When it comes to the end, dementia seems to draw the short straw because while no doctor would be happy to see a patient writhing in pain and confusion while cancer ate away at their organs, they seem to be quite comfortable to see a person writhing away in pain and confusion while dementia slowly kills their brain cells, finally leaving them unable to swallow or talk.

Many people believe that if you have an enduring power of attorney for your relative then you have the right to request medical staff to withhold treatment. You don't. You can request a 'do not resuscitate' order (DNR) and you can deny them antibiotics if they get a life-threatening infection like pneumonia. But you can't stop them being medicated to save their lives, like the insulin my mother was given, or the drip she was put on when she developed kidney problems and wouldn't drink.

Staff will also cajole your relative to eat even when they refuse food. I have seen nurses in my mother's stroke ward wake up and feed a woman who lay in bed barely moving and barely conscious for a week. She clearly didn't want the food, but they got it down her anyway. The doctors will order this because it's good medical practice — and a requirement under the current law — to keep patients alive if you can. Not necessarily because it is in the patient's best interests to be kept alive.

As I wrote this New Zealanders were about to have the chance to vote on the End of Life Choice Act in a binding referendum during the 2020 election. The official figures released afterwards showed that 65.1 per cent voted in favour of the Act, which means it will come into effect in November 2021. From that time, those of us who meet certain criteria will have the option of legally requesting help to end our lives — either by doing so ourselves (euthanasia) or with the help of a doctor (assisted dying). To be eligible, you need to be suffering from a terminal illness that is likely to end your life within six months. There are further hurdles for eligibility. You need to be in 'an advanced state of irreversible decline in physical capability', experience unbearable suffering 'that cannot be relieved in a manner that they consider tolerable', and be competent to make an informed decision about dying. You will also need the approval of two doctors, but you will not need sworn witness statements from family members.

This Act would not have helped Mum. The doctors who were responsible for her care chose not to let her die — mainly because she could eat, and under the law that meant she had to be kept alive no matter what state she was in.

• • •

Since Mum's death I've realised that we were woefully unprepared for handling her care on that day when the doctors told my brother that she was to live. We simply let them decide that she would be a burden on either the taxpayer or my dad's savings for as many months or years as it took for her to die. We never questioned it, disputed it or took action.

Although my mother had written a 'living will' years before, which stated her desire not to live in the way she was being forced to live, at the time of her stroke no one could find it, and every time I mentioned it to the hospital staff it was dismissed as not having any legality. That is true. Anything written before 2005 is generally discounted as being a load of rubbish. I have since discovered that had we been prepared, we could have legally requested that the doctors withhold her insulin there and then and let her die from an underlying illness, her diabetes. For a start, we could have insisted on a meeting with the doctors who were caring for her and our family. This was never offered to us, which seems incredible to me. To be fair, they may have offered such a meeting to my brother, but he has no memory of that. It appears that here was a woman whose future was in the hands of a couple of doctors, yet they were not interested in talking formally to that woman's family.

I would like to say that I remember the face or name of one of the doctors who cared for Mum, but I can't. There were about five different doctors, and not one of them ever suggested that my family had any say in what was going on with her care. I felt very much that this was their domain and we would obey their rules. One woman doctor was good at listening, but I never felt she was taking any action on anything I told her.

If we had had such a meeting we could have produced what is called an advance directive (AD) document signed by Mum and a witness, and updated annually to show that she had mental competence when she signed it. For extra measure, we could have included a mental capacity form signed by Mum's doctor to indicate that she was fully aware that she was signing the AD. And when she got dementia, another note from her doctor confirming this.

I learned all of this in the book I had initially dismissed as a 'self-published nightmare', along with information from a charity in the UK called Advance Decisions Assistance. All of this information led me back to New Zealand, where I found that this was something everyone in this country is free to do as well. We had just never known about it.

Mum's AD would have included her wish to not be given CPR, ventilation, a feeding tube, antibiotics, chemotherapy, dialysis or insulin, statins, blood pressure medication, angina medication or stroke medication. It would also have included consent to treatment to alleviate pain or distress. And we should have made sure that she wrote a statement outlining her reasons why she was requesting this. Had we produced this document, the doctors at the hospital would have been legally obliged to take notice of this wish and Mum would have been dead in days thanks to the withdrawal of insulin alone. According to the New Zealand Medical Association, 'doctors must act in the incapacitated patient's best interests. Evidence of an informed advance decision, whether oral or written, should be taken into account when deciding what is in the individual patient's best interests.'

So there was a way around Mum having to rot away in a care home for ten weeks in a state that was clearly not 'in the individual patient's best interests'. But because we had never come across this situation before, we were unprepared and I feel that we let Mum down. I had tried to discuss Mum's long-term care with my parents, but had not got very far. Had I known that an AD was an option I would certainly have made them aware and encouraged them to sign one.

I felt bad about this for a while, but then I realised that not many people sit down one day and think, 'Right, I'd better make sure I know how to kill my mother if things get weird.' Even talking to friends about this issue highlighted how little anyone really wants to do this kind of mega-planning for death. One friend whose mother is in her eighties and in excellent health said, 'Oh I don't think we'll need to do an advance directive. She'll not lose her mental capacity before she goes.'

But what if she has a half-stroke, and is left the way my mum was in a care home for a year? Wouldn't you want to withdraw any medication she was on to reduce her high blood pressure or the chance of another stroke that could end her misery? Even the healthiest, most active, brightest and most aware old people can be incapacitated mentally, quite quickly.

I will also say that I feel the doctors caring for Mum were no doubt under a lot of pressure to get her out of the acute ward and stop costing the taxpayer money to keep her there. I know that they sent our friend Frank out of the ward too soon and he was back in there with a broken hip because of it. I do not understand, however, why they didn't do us the courtesy of having a meeting to discuss Mum's future, and why they couldn't at least sign her off for palliative care to die in a rest home. I guess if they'd had the AD as supporting paperwork they would have been able to protect themselves from a lawsuit or similar.

• • •

According to our Ministry of Health, an advance care plan should 'be written in the knowledge that it could have legal authority. Patients should be reassured that their advance care plan will be referred to in future if they are unable to speak for themselves. Advance care plans need to be regularly reviewed and updated as and when situations change.'

So far there has been no legal push-back on the use of an AD, so your doctor should have no qualms about following it. Doctors can only refuse to follow a patient's wishes in an AD if they believe the patient was not competent to make the advance directive (a good reason to update it every year, along with a yearly competency statement signed by your doctor), the patient didn't make the decision of their own free will, they weren't sufficiently informed to make the decision, their present circumstances are different to those anticipated, or the advance directive is out of date. All these things need to be taken into account when you are writing your AD, which is why it is helpful to write a summary at the end covering all these possible reasons why a doctor might deny you and your family your rights.

You should also discuss the AD with your doctor and get them to lodge it in your medical file with a note from them in support. They will know what to do. You should also share it with your family members and close friends, keep a copy in the glove box of your car, and give it to the hospital if you are having an operation. The more people who know about it, the better.

I got my father to draw up an AD, and asked him to run it past his doctor who talked to him about it, made a few changes and then signed it, too. She specialises in end-of-life care, so I knew we were in good hands. I adopted her changes into my AD, which I've included at the end of this book, along with some links for downloading AD templates and doing further research. You may also find that some care homes have advance directive forms ready and waiting for you to sign — but you will need to ask for them.

• • •

Am I angry that some doctors played God and decided to push Mum off onto a care home to be kept alive, instead of letting her die as was her wish? Absolutely. I am furious.

The sad situation is that many families will be just like ours at that time in the hospital — wanting their family member to be set free to die, knowing that their family member wanted that to happen, but unable to negotiate their way around the medical staff to allow it to happen.

I advise anyone whose family has a history of dementia, Alzheimer's, mental illness, stroke or any illness that might mean they become mentally incapacitated to arrange one of these documents as soon as possible. If there is any chance that in your future you might lose your mental capacity, and you have other illnesses that you could easily die of if treatment is withheld (such as diabetes or a high stroke risk), then this document will help you die instead of living in a care home for months or years, out of your mind and paralysed, and unable to do anything about it.

CHAPTER 20

Lost father found

O nly those who have experienced it know what it is like to have a parent in the world whom they have never met. For some, I'm sure it is a constant in their lives — wondering whether they look like their missing parent, whether there is a half-sibling or two out there, and what talents or illnesses they might have inherited. For others, like my mother, the missing parent was just that . . . missing. From her life and from her thoughts. Her biological father simply didn't exist for her.

Mum had a good relationship with her birth mother Eileen, especially in her late teens and early adult life. Dad remembers that after meeting Mum at that party with the beer under the bed, she was off to Whanganui the next day to spend time with Eileen. Mum made sure that Dad knew that just in case he was planning to get in touch for a date or anything like that. She would be away for three days. Just in case he was wondering.

There is a picture of Mum and Eileen sitting next to each other where they are both leaning forward with their elbows on their knees. That's about the only similarity anyone could find between the two — the fact that they sat the same way. Mum didn't look like Eileen at all, and had a different personality.

Whenever I asked about her father, Mum would tell me the little she knew. That his name was either Larsen or Lawson; something like that. He was a farmer in Taranaki and had quite a few children. That was it. When I suggested about ten years ago that it might be quite a simple process to find him and her half-siblings, she shut the door on that.

'He's dead. Don't bother.'

This made me immediately suspicious, because if she knew that he was dead, then she knew who he was and what his name was. I felt that she was being deliberately vague to throw me off the scent.

Mum's impression of her father was not a great one, which is understandable as by all accounts he may have raped her mother, or at the very least taken advantage of her. I'm sure that in such a small place as Taranaki she would have heard all about him, but perhaps she didn't really want to have anything to do with him or his offspring. However, I was consumed with curiosity. What did he look like? Do any of my children look like him? Did I have aunts, uncles and cousins?

Then I got it into my head that Mum was quite possibly part Māori. She had dark hair and slightly olive skin. Maybe it wasn't a Larsen/Lawson who had raped her mother but instead a teenage romance with one of the Māori farm-hands? This thought delighted me. I have Māori children, and through them I have been able to learn and love their culture and, yes, may have appropriated quite a bit of it into my own life. I am one of those middle-aged white women who wears a greenstone taonga. But it was given to me. Apparently that's okay. I may be wrong, and if so I apologise for any cultural appropriation.

I realised that if Mum was part-Māori we needed to know her tribe and affiliations, which would be very beneficial for my children to be aware of.

A few years ago, I was offered a couple of DNA kits from Ancestry.com in return for writing a story (which I never did, but I am now). I knew immediately that one of these would go to Mum. We could finally find out what was going on in her lineage. We knew Eileen was mainly Irish, but what about Mum's other DNA? Where did she get her looks from if it wasn't Eileen? At the time Mum was a willing participant, but by the time the results came back in 2016 her dementia had started to set in and she had no interest at all in either her results or finding her father. What her results showed was that she was Irish, which we knew from Eileen's Gallagher side, but the rest was a big whack of Norwegian DNA — and nothing to indicate any Māori heritage. So Larsen/Lawson it was for Dad of the Year.

Because of Mum's negative response, I gave up on the hunt for her father and logged out of Ancestry.com. I decided it could wait until she had died, and then maybe I would take another look. I didn't want to stress Mum out by pursuing it then.

• • •

A few months after Mum's death in July 2019, I logged back on to Ancestry.com and got a big shock. There in my inbox were emails from a family who had found a direct link with my mum's DNA. It took me a matter of 24 hours and a few emails to find out that Mum's father was a man called Rupert Larsen, who was a farmer in the Taranaki and had six children; five boys and a girl.

Mum's and my DNA had scored a direct hit with some of my Larsen cousins who had also put their DNA samples into Ancestry.com. Fortunately my cousins are quite good at working genealogy out, and had narrowed it down to the fact that Elis must be their aunty. To confirm this, they asked Rupert's only known surviving child, Joy, to do a DNA test and got a direct hit as Mum's half-sister. The Larsens had been trying to make contact since May 2018, but because I had stayed logged out of Ancestry.com there had been no reply from me. When I finally made contact, they were absolutely delighted. We put all the pieces of the jigsaw together and swapped photos. Mum looked a lot like her half-sister Joy, but not a lot like her father Rupert.

I now had twenty new cousins of whom seventeen were alive, and they were all very welcoming, and quite excited I think to have made this discovery. None of them had had any idea that there was another child out there, although they had heard of Rupert's reputation as a bit of a womaniser. He and his brother Rex were known to be 'ladies' men'.

'When he died,' said one of my new cousins, 'we were waiting to hear about all the other children he had fathered around Taranaki, but nothing came out.'

It was clear that all of my new cousins loved their grandfather Rupert, and knew him as a kind and generous man who was also extremely charming — which was what made him popular with the ladies. But now some of them were starting to think that he might have had another side to him. Together we worked out that as Rupert was born on 24 February 1900, he would have been 32 years old when Eileen became pregnant with Mum. We also realised that Rupert's wife Beryl was in her ninth month of pregnancy — with Joy — when Mum was conceived. And I knew that Eileen had just turned seventeen around about the time she conceived.

How long had the relationship been going on before she got pregnant, we wondered. Was she sixteen when they started having sex, or could she have been younger? Eileen had been working for the family since she was fourteen. We recalled that in those times the woman always got the blame for any extra-marital relations, but Eileen was very young and Rupert was an adult of 32 and a family man. There was no other conclusion to be drawn but that Rupert was not a great guy to have done this.

In the early 1930s, Rupert had a job as a mountain ranger and tour guide, and with his wife Beryl they managed the old North Egmont House on Mt Taranaki, a historic camphouse nearly 1000 metres up the mountain. There are reports in *The New Zealand Herald* of Rupert being quite the ranger and hero in one case where he helped retrieve the body of a 21-year-old tramper who had collapsed and died on the mountain. But this idyllic lifestyle on Mt Taranaki was to end in 1932, supposedly because Rupert's carrying-on with the ladies didn't go down well with his bosses.

I found this excerpt in the personal columns of the *Waikato Times*, published on 27 June 1932.

> *As an expression of appreciation of their popular custodianship of the old North Egmont House, and their many services to visitors to the mountain in a variety of capacities, Mr and Mrs Rupert Larsen, who are leaving the mountain to go back to Mr Larsen's farm at Uruti, were the guest of honour at a Taranaki Alpine Club social in New Plymouth when they were presented with a large framed portrait of Mt Egmont as a memento of their association with the club.*

So Rupert and Beryl left the mountain the year before Mum was born. This meant that she must have been conceived while Rupert was back on the family farm in Urutī. Urutī is in northern Taranaki and is so isolated, hilly, moody and mist-covered that it was chosen by film director Vincent Ward as the setting for his dark 1984 film *Vigil*. Hollywood later came to Urutī to film *The Last Samurai*.

Eventually Rupert bought a farm in Puke Road and the family moved in there. However, whenever necessary for farming tasks, Rupert would stay in the cabin at the back farm in Pehu. Mum's half-sister Joy has lovely memories of riding her pony with him to the back farm, staying in the cabin and helping with the work there. That cabin may have been where Eileen got pregnant. However, Eileen definitely did not go with the family as their housekeeper to Uruti, so how she and Rupert met up on the back farm in Pehu to conceive Mum is a mystery.

You can imagine that Rupert's wife Beryl was devastated when she discovered that Eileen was having a baby. The subsequent paternity case taken up by Eileen's parents named Rupert as the defendant, but also, rather surprisingly, his wife Beryl as a defence witness. It could be that Beryl was sure that the two could not have met out in the back blocks of Urutī, miles from the mountain and from New Plymouth where Eileen may have been living, and therefore he couldn't possibly be the father.

Beryl's brother was a lawyer and acted on their behalf in the case. When they lost, Beryl refused to speak to him for many years. If only they had had DNA tests back then; this would have saved Beryl the embarrassment of supporting her husband in court and alienating her brother. Beryl had baby Joy at the time, and it must have been emotionally draining and upsetting to have to put on her good clothes and turn up at court where she would have to tell the judge that she believed her husband was a good man who would never get a young girl pregnant. She would also have had to look at that girl, Eileen, who had worked in her kitchen and beside her as they cleaned and cooked and looked after the children. They might have been good friends and got on well.

Meanwhile, Eileen at seventeen would have had to stand up in court and point the finger at a man that she may have loved in her teenage way. Perhaps this was a relationship that was full of romance, where Rupert bought her gifts and idolised her. Or it could have been a more sordid one of pressure and manipulation. Either way, Eileen would have been embarrassed and shamed by having to appear in court.

I have spent quite some time thinking about Rupert's ability to deny paternity to the point of turning up at court and bringing his wife with him to attest to his innocence. Did he paint Eileen as a trouble-making fantasist? Probably.

I decided that I wanted to visit Joy, who lives in Queensland; there was a need for me to sit with her and look into her eyes, which resembled my mother's so closely. From Joy's daughter I learned that she was musical, like my mum, and also a feminist. She had been a member of the National Council of Women and raised her three daughters to be strong, independent women. I haven't managed to see Joy yet, because of the Covid-19 border closures, but I hope to soon.

It appears that because of Eileen and the pregnancy, Joy might have suffered at the hands of her mother Beryl. As the only girl in a family of six children, she was treated like a princess by Rupert and her brothers. But Beryl was quite unkind to her and could get nasty at times. She also talked about Eileen Gallagher in angry and disparaging terms, which was understandable.

There is a great picture of Rupert in the Puke Ariki museum in Taranaki, aged 43 and wearing military uniform. He and his sons (my uncles) Terence (then eighteen), Colin (sixteen) and Albert (twenty) had all had their pictures taken together at Swainson Studios on 24 June 1943. Rupert never actually went to war. Men were conscripted up to the age of 45, and Rupert trained as a soldier and was part of the Home Guard, which is why he was in uniform. He was also a farmer, and food production was considered an integral part of the war effort. By 1945, the last year of the war, farmers made up a third of the men who had been kept out of the armed forces to work at home.

Rupert died on 8 May 1976 when I was aged fourteen, so I could have met him had Mum made contact. Whether I would have liked him or not, I'm not sure.

CHAPTER 21

Good grief

On 14 January 2020, nearly six months after my mother's death, I found myself trying to find a park on Jervois Road in Ponsonby, Auckland. I couldn't find one, and before I knew it I was in floods of tears. Uncontrollable sobs that felt like they were coming out of every organ of my body, all having a good old squeeze and getting rid of the pus that had formed in them. Just a few days earlier I had been having a massage at my favourite Thai massage clinic and had burst into tears, something I had never done in all my years of receiving my favourite treat. The therapist asked me if I was hot, presuming that I was sweating. I said, no, just crying. She continued the massage, but every few minutes dabbed a tissue under my eyes to take away the tears. I cried for the full two hours of the session.

I was actually trying to find a park so that I could see my counsellor because of my constant crying. It wasn't because I was missing my mother, or pining for our relationship, or because I was sad. I didn't miss having my mother in my life at all. If anything, my life was so much better without her in it. I no longer had to deal with her moods, her attacks, her drinking, her jealousy. It was true that the past few years while she had been demented were much more pleasant, but I was dealing with a good 55 years of unpleasantness before that. It was a relief to have it gone. But I was wracked with constant negative thoughts about her. Never any nice ones; always the horrible ones, replaying over and over, night and day. No matter how hard I tried, the events I've described earlier in the book insisted on having their time again. There I was in the yellow-jersey halter dress at the party, being insulted by my mother for having small tits. There I was in the short tassel dress on the cruise ship, being called a slut. It felt like my grief was one long bad movie and I couldn't leave the cinema. I badly wanted to get up and walk out of that movie and into the next-door cinema where they were playing *Oh How I Loved My Mother and Miss Her So*, but there was to be none of that.

On another level, I felt that I was being just like my mum — basing the quality of my life on a list of half a dozen horrible things that had happened to me at the hands of my mother.

Initially, my grief for Mum was fairly non-existent. I was relieved that she had died and was not suffering. I was relieved that I didn't have to worry about her and try to make sure she was getting the best care possible. I was relieved, if I'm honest, to not have her in my life anymore. Up until the last two years, her presence in my life had been something to bear, not to enjoy.

About two months after she died, I went through a particularly bizarre week where I realised that I had essentially killed my mother by withholding antibiotics. I talked to Dad about it, I talked to Paul about it, I talked to my kids about it, and I talked to my friends about it.

'You realise I actually killed her,' I would say.

There really is no response to that, but a few were ventured. Mainly people said that I had just allowed nature to take its course, and that is not the same as taking a knife and stabbing her to death.

In the end I guess I worked through it, but the fact remains. I killed her.

• • •

I constantly compared myself with my friends who have lovely mothers and would grieve the nice way when their mothers were gone, because their mothers had been present in their lives with unconditional love, helped when their babies were born, in fact helped whenever my friends needed it.

I read an article about comedian Billy Connolly, who sank into a major depression for three months after his abusive father died. Like me, he could not stop the bad memories playing over and over. Billy's father had been terribly abusive; my mother wasn't that bad, so why the bloody drama?

I talked to my youngest daughter, Pearl, about how surprised I was to be having these bad memories, but I guessed that Mum occupied a part of me all my life and that part had gone. Pearl said, 'Maybe sometimes it's less about who the person was, and more about being sad about the person they should have been.' Which was incredibly insightful.

I told Paul that I now understood why people used to wear black when they were grieving. It sent a clear message that you were sensitive and ailing. I wish I had a T-shirt saying 'Leave me alone, I'm not up to being nice today.'

I figured that it would all ease eventually, but when I hit six months and it was still going on, I saw my counsellor. She confirmed that this sort of reaction is common when a parent has hurt a child. We discussed my relationship with my mother. I listed the memories that I was having and she did a wonderful thing by putting it all into perspective.

The reality of my relationship with my mother was that for most of my early childhood, it was fine. Mum fed and clothed and cared for her little girl. The trouble really started in my early teens when I turned into a woman physically, started answering back and in her eyes became a threat — so from about the age of twelve until I left home at sixteen. So there were four years under her roof that were quite destructive. After that, Mum's behaviour was annoying and hurtful but not damaging, because

I could get away from it and live my own life. I could decide not to talk to her for months and years, if I wanted to, which in fact I did to protect myself and my family.

So really I was dealing with four years, that's all. Four years out of my 57 years of life.

Somehow that made it all a lot easier and helped me not to overthink things. In my grief I was focusing on some things that had happened to me which were awful, but then there were the other 53 years which were pretty good and safe — the years when I fell in love and had children and created my own family, without passing on any of Elis's bad mothering habits.

Next we set about erasing my reaction to those bad memories by using a technique called EFT (emotional freedom therapy) tapping. I had to drag up every memory that was haunting me, then tap various pressure points on my face (think acupressure). Slowly, the memory will fade and you end up having little or no reaction to it.

I got home up north, took myself for a walk on the beach with the dogs, sat on a log in the sun and worked through the bad memories every day. Tap tap tapping, slowly reducing their enormity in my head. It took me about a week to get through them all and then, just like that, I was free of it. In another week I felt the most normal I had felt since Mum had her stroke at Easter the year before, and finally I started easing myself out of grief.

• • •

I had only had one experience of grief before, when my three-month-old daughter Virginia died of cot death in 1992, and that was completely different. It was completely dominated by the misery of missing someone and the 'what if?' questions you have around how things might have been if she had lived. No wonder I was so confused.

There is a school of thought, held by Paul and his family who are funeral directors and know what they're talking about, that having a funeral is an essential part of the grieving process. At the time it's the last thing you feel like organising, but the ritual of it, the sharing of grief with friends and family, and even sending the coffin off into the ground or into the incinerator is important. I think they are right — but we didn't do that, because it wasn't what Mum wanted. Instead, we simply had her cremated and then had a memorial five months later with a small group of family and friends. Dad was determined that there would be no speeches, no fuss. Just a simple remembrance with some food and drinks and some photos. It was pretty awful, to be honest. I appreciated the efforts everyone made to come to our house in the Hokianga, but I hated every minute of it and was glad when everyone left. My grief did not make me a better person.

With no funeral to organise, I had made the decision to still go on a trip to Europe just a few days after Mum had died. The trip had been planned for two years, and was a bit unusual in that Paul was the tour leader, something he regularly did for a travel company. This holiday would be shared with about twenty other people, some of them quite elderly. Dad had encouraged us to go even though he was still quite frail and under the weather. I arranged for my brother and some friends to keep an eye on him, and left him to it. To be honest, I needed a bit of a break from him, too, as I was now his primary relationship in the world.

Part of me thought that a holiday spent in my favourite place in the world, Italy, would be just the tonic, so I packed my bags. I carefully slipped Mum's opal and diamond engagement ring onto my right ring finger. It was one of the first things I saw when I was born and it's glinted at me my whole life. It sat on my finger and stared at me, shocked and dismayed at the new turn of events and the new finger. I fiddled with it, I twisted it around and around, and by the end of two long flights to Europe we had got used to each other.

Then I added jetlag to grief and found myself crying in all sorts of odd places — overlooking the Grand Canal in Venice, standing in a queue at the supermarket in Santa Margherita Ligure, swimming at a beach in Malta.

I don't recommend travel as a way to grieve; it doesn't work. It seems like a good idea to have a change of scene, to get away from it all and start afresh. But after three months of worry and stress and seeing your mum suffer the indignities of being stranded alone and fearful in a care home, you need to be grounded and secure. You need your home and your bed. You need your cat on your lap and your dogs at your feet. You need to hug your kids, your dad and your husband for hours. You need to surround yourself with the familiar, not the foreign. Instead, I was in Lake Como — which was gorgeous, but not home. I was helping Paul with his hosting duties, but I had just spent three months caring for an elderly and confused woman, and it appeared we also had a few on this trip. I was caring again, and this time for people I barely knew. My veneer of politeness was incredibly thin.

By the time we reached Venice, about a week into the trip, I couldn't stop crying. I spent one night just lying in my hotel room crying and looking out at the Grand Canal; actually not a bad place to spend the night crying.

I felt like I had no control over this thing, and decided that I should go home. I also realised that I couldn't do this alone. I don't think grieving is something you should do in isolation. So I asked Paul to forgo spending the morning on a tour with the group and instead spend the morning in Venice with me, and that did it. Slowly the urge to cry subsided and I realised that I could keep going.

We then boarded a cruise ship and I got really sick: full-blown flu with aching muscles, fever and a cough. So I read a lot, finished writing the book I was working on, and that was about it. I could have been on a Pacific Island and achieved the same result, and saved a lot of money.

• • •

When we returned home I then had to sort out Mum's things. Dad couldn't face it. I persuaded him to spend some time at his caravan, and I would clear Mum's belongings out of the cottage while he was gone. He was quite happy to let me do that. In fact, he needed me to do that.

But there was a problem. Every time I smelled Mum on her clothes or in her chaotic drawers of bits and pieces, I wanted to throw up. I would have to drop everything and run from the cottage to breathe in huge gulps of fresh air. I couldn't do it; I couldn't touch her stuff. In the end Paul did it with me, putting everything into boxes and bags as I directed from the door of the bedroom where I couldn't smell anything.

I have no idea why that was, nor do I want to know. It was yet another strange and weird thing that happened to me because of my mother. Your sense of smell can take you straight to an emotion, so that was obviously what was happening.

I washed and dried all Mum's clothes, then packed up the good ones for the op shop and threw the rest out. Her jewellery I sorted and saved for her grandchildren. Probably the saddest thing was throwing out her bridge club ID badge, which she had pinned to her clothes every time she headed off to play. In her later years it was probably her proudest possession.

• • •

The dream about my mother finally came, as I knew it would. I dreamt that I was at my ex-husband's house and the phone rang. He said it was Mum. Reluctantly I went over to pick up the receiver — which is exactly what I used to do — and she was on the other end asking me why she had a memorial card about our baby Virginia's death day. I reminded her that she had died in 1992, and she said: 'Oh yes, she's here.'

Then she turned up at the house and said she was going to drive away. I told her she couldn't drive anymore, but then I realised she was dead, so I said: 'Well if you want to, then off you go.'

That was it, really. I woke up crying my eyes out. I guess because of the connection between her and Virginia.

CHAPTER 22

Living with Dad

So now it is just Dad next door. And what a joy it is to have him there. Slowly but surely in the year following Mum's death, my father emerged from his weakened, sad and shut-down state back into the man he was before her death — and then into a man I'd never really seen before.

After 65 years of marriage with Mum, I believe that Dad has a newfound freedom. A chance to be himself without criticism or shaming from Mum. He's funny, chatty and witty all at once and quite a lot, because no one is interrupting him or shutting him up as my mother used to do. I always knew he had it in him; I just never really heard him say these things out loud.

He's now 88, and every day he does something on the property in the Hokianga, whether it's hopping on his ride-on mower to do the lawns, building a set of shelves for the garage or putting together a garden seat for the orchard. He enjoys cooking his own dinner every night, preferring simple meals of meat and three veg with ice cream to finish. He has a couple of wines a night, and sits in his La-Z-Boy chair and tells himself how lucky he is to be here. He takes off to his caravan in the Bay of Plenty every few months to enjoy a few weeks of staring at a different sea view and keeping in touch with his mates down there.

Slowly he's adjusted to the fact that his body is frail and he can no longer lift heavy things, so he asks us to do it. He's developed a little garden outside his cottage which he keeps a close eye on, and he's become quite dotty about one of our cats, Peggy, who only has three legs. Dad has decided that he is her exclusive carer.

But the best thing is that me and my dad can be with each other and enjoy each other's company without the constant inter-ference and jealousy of my mother. We can sit in companionable silence, or chat about the weather. We can spend hours discussing at length the hens, the dogs, the garden, the cats, Covid-19, Jacinda Ardern (fabulous), the National Party (dreadful), and the terrible state of the media these days. We can hop in the boat and go fishing. He can drive me to the airport in Kerikeri when I have a plane to catch. I am so lucky to have him here and I know that I will look back on this time as being a very special gift, however long it lasts.

We talk about Mum sometimes, but not a lot, which surprises me. For someone who loomed so large in both of our lives, you would think we would have a lot to say about her. But we don't. I think we prefer to forget a lot of it.

The other day we took the boat out and placed Mum's ashes on the little island that sits out the front of our place. There were no prayers said. Dad simply scattered her ashes and said, 'There you are, Elis. Back where you came from.'

Then we went fishing and he caught a three-kilogram snapper.

I've told him a lot of stuff about my childhood that he simply wasn't aware of. Just about everything I've written in this book came as a complete surprise to him, mainly because of his remarkable capacity to forgive and forget, erasing any bad experiences immediately from his memory.

And there are two memories I shared with him about Mum which happened in those delightful few years she was with us here in the Hokianga as dementia slowly took hold.

One day, as I was opening the gate for Dad's car as they set off on one of Mum's drives, my mother rolled down her window and beckoned me to her side of the car.

I went over and leaned in.

'I'm so proud of you,' she said, grinning from ear to ear.

Later, when she was lying in hospital post-stroke and deeply unhappy, she beckoned me to lean in to her again.

'I love you,' she said.

Finally.

Helpful hints and tips

Here I've gathered a few things I found helpful when talking with my demented mother, as well as the vitally important information about advance directives.

How to talk to an older person (with or without dementia)
A few years ago, Paul's step-mother Valmai became quite unhappy; possibly she was in the first stages of the dementia she lives with now.

Visits became arduous affairs where she fired one negative arrow after another about the state of her life. We've all seen it. Someone who is unhappy that they've ended up without the ability to drive, play bridge, get out and about, and is therefore feeling quite lonely. Who wouldn't be unhappy with this state of affairs?

After one particularly harrowing visit to Valmai I went away and became determined to work out what to do so that we wouldn't stop visiting because it was too hard. I know this often happens with family, who think that the old person is being such a pain they won't visit. Don't do that. In many cases you are one of their few lifelines to the outside world.

What I found was a magnificent technique that we still use with Valmai today.

Instead of trying to fix every negative, just agree. It's called reflective listening. So when someone says, 'I hate my life, I am so lonely,' don't say, 'Oh come on now, cheer up, chook. You need to be more positive.'

Instead, say: 'I know it's hard and this isn't what you expected to happen to you. You must be very lonely.'

They will then say: 'You are so right.'

And then miraculously the thought goes away and the conversation is clear for you to start introducing nice things like, 'Wow look at your roses, aren't they flourishing?' And away you go talking about roses and sharing the joy.

When someone is deeply unhappy, they really just want to be taken seriously and be listened to. They don't want to be jollied along and have you fix the problem, which in most cases is unfixable anyway. Instead, say their sadness back to them and you'll be amazed at how that makes such a big difference.

Paul talks to his step-mother regularly in the care home, and some of those days she is down and unhappy and crying. Who wouldn't be, stuck in a care home having lost your ability to remember what day it is, what time it is and the fact that you are visited often by your large family? Valmai feels lonely, rejected, neglected and sad.

I listened to Paul do this reflective listening while we were all in the first Covid-19 lockdown and she couldn't have visitors. I marvelled at his skill and patience. If you have dementia, you don't remember every day when you wake up that you are in lockdown. Most of the time Paul and Valmai would end up talking about the sunshine and the dinner she was going to have, but sometimes it would still be pretty depressing an hour later. I would hear Paul gently say: 'It must be so hard for you feeling like you are stuck in your room with nothing fun to do.'

Then he would introduce some new stuff: 'I hear you went out in the van for a drive the other day, what did you see?'

The other thing you absolutely must try to do if you have an old person in your life is ring them often, every day if you can. It's hard, it can be frustrating and it's repetitive, but that call takes them out of themselves for a little while and, quite frankly, that is the least you can do for them. If you can visit them every day, then do so. It's actually not that much to ask to sit and have a coffee for half an hour if you have time. And if you don't have an old person in your life, then maybe find someone at your local care home who would appreciate a visitor.

Personally I find Valmai challenging because she has a direct channel into my heart and when she cries, I cry. Years ago she fell ill and was in hospital for a while over Christmas, and as there was no other family in town it fell to Paul and me to look after her. I spent hours with her in that hospital room and we became very close. Now when I visit her, if she looks at me and starts crying I am beside myself and cry along with her, which is absolutely no use to anyone. So sometimes I just let Paul do the visit. But I am working on some new techniques for being strong enough to sit and reflectively listen without needing my handkerchief, and hers.

Other tips for people with dementia

- Give them boxes and bags full of stuff. Mum used to love opening up a shopping bag and 'discovering' what was inside. I would plant shopping bags in her bedroom filled with cooking magazines, cheap jewellery, a handkerchief, a lipstick and some perfume. All stuff you can get cheaply from op shops and chemists. This could keep her busy for ages as she would take them out one by one and place them on the bed. She'd then put them all away and put the bag carefully on the floor to be rediscovered tomorrow — or even ten minutes later.

- Sit with photo albums. Taking someone with dementia through old family albums is nice. Sometimes they will have no memory of an event but be really pleased to see it. Other times they will have all the memory there and will tell you stories about people you never heard of before.

- Play games or do jigsaws. The mind is progressively shrinking, but that doesn't mean that parts of it aren't still great at playing games like Scrabble or cards or doing jigsaws. Some days it won't be that great, but on others it will be just like it used to be. It really is worth taking the time to do these things with them.

- Play with toys. My mother wasn't particularly keen on this, but some people do like cuddling teddies or dressing dolls — or murdering them, as in the case of one woman in the care home I saw. Either way, it's worth a try if you have a kid's doll somewhere with some clothes they can put on and off.

- Play music. Music can be very calming. I knew my mother would respond to classical music, although listening to music wasn't something she and my father usually liked to do. When she was in the care home I put a radio in there and tuned it to Concert FM, thinking she would love to listen to it, but the next time I visited it was turned off. It's still worth a try, though.

- Watch TV together. Mum gave up on the TV quite early on in her dementia, but others like it, especially wildlife documentaries or children's shows. An Agatha Christie murder mystery won't cut it anymore, but nice pictures or a concert will always be a good distraction.

Advance directives

Here are some useful links I have found.

- The New Zealand Medical Association has a complete planning booklet that you can print off. It can be found at: **nzma.org.nz/patients/advance-directive**

- There is a template and guide for a New Zealand advance directive at:
hqsc.govt.nz/assets/ACP/PR/ACP_Plan_print_.pdf

- The website **adassistance.org.uk** is British, but has some great advice on making sure that your advance directive is as good and clear as it can be.

And here is my own advance directive form:

ADVANCE DIRECTIVE FORM FOR:
WENDYL MORDUE NISSEN

Address: ....

....

Date of birth: ....

Health number: ....

GP: ....

Statement:

If I become permanently unable to make or communicate decisions about my medical treatment, I wish to REFUSE all treatments/interventions which may prolong my life.
This refusal includes (but is not limited to):

- Cardio-pulmonary resuscitation (CPR)
- Ventilation
- Treatments designed to maintain or replace a vital bodily function (such as a heart pacemaker)
- A feeding tube
- Antibiotics given for a potentially life-threatening infection
- Specialised treatments for a particular condition (such as chemotherapy, dialysis or insulin)
- Other current treatments/medications

I maintain this refusal even if it shortens my life.

If I refuse food and/or drink by mouth, I also refuse repeated attempts to feed/hydrate me or being persuaded or cajoled to eat or drink — even if this refusal shortens my life.

I do consent to treatment to alleviate pain or distress, even if it shortens my life.

I confirm that information about the risks, consequences and treatment options of my decision have been explained to me.

Wendyl Nissen

Signature: ....

Date: ....

Witness name and address: ....

....

Witness signature: ....

Date: ....

Updated/reconsidered/endorsed on ....

Updated/reconsidered/endorsed on ....

Updated/reconsidered/endorsed on ....

Advance values statement:

From May to July 2019 I watched my mother exist in a vegetative state in a care home because the doctors who treated her stroke in Whangārei Hospital decided she should live even though she was unable to talk, was paralysed, incontinent, demented and could not feed herself.

I knew that she would have wanted to die and this would have been easily achieved by withdrawing her insulin and the other nine medications she was on to keep her alive.

Watching this bright, intelligent woman who had been suffering from dementia for two years half-live for those three months before pneumonia finally killed her made me determined that the same would not happen to me.

Should I lose the ability to communicate for myself I want to be left to die, and helped with some good pain relief. That is why I have signed this form and kept it updated.

Under no circumstances am I not competent to make this advance directive. I have made this decision of my own free will, I am sufficiently informed to make this decision, and my present circumstances are the same as those anticipated.

You are legally obliged to put this advance directive into action. If you refuse to act on this advance directive my family will sue you. You can be sure of it.

Author's note

For a large part of my mother's life, the 'Ladies at the Bridge Club' meant a lot to her. Mum was a great bridge player who often won tournaments. She regarded her membership at the club as something very special, and placed a lot of social status on it.

Mum was never one of those mothers who clipped my articles and put them in a scrapbook or watched and listened to my work on television and radio. She once told me that she would never be one of those 'fawning mothers who make their lives all about their children', and made a point of letting me know she hadn't seen my work. When someone would say to her, 'Oh, I've just realised you are Wendyl Nissen's mother!', she hated it and would tell me so because it took the light off her and onto me.

But the Ladies at the Bridge Club did read, watch and listen to me, and would often tell Mum about my various bits and pieces that were out there in the public eye. Then I would be in trouble for not telling her, because she would have to feign interest and pretend that she was indeed one of those fawning mothers, for fear of being criticised and judged. She was often embarrassed by things I had done that the ladies seemed to revel in informing her about in vivid detail. She lived in fear of those ladies, I think in a school-yard-bullying way. On the one hand she was a brilliant bridge player with a daughter in the media, but on the other she could be taken down in a second, in public, surrounded by her friends, by one of those ladies.

If you are one of those Ladies from the Bridge Club and have picked up this book so that you can scorn, laugh at or gossip about my mother, please don't. Please read these words with respect and understanding.

About the author

Wendyl Nissen is a journalist, broadcaster and former magazine editor who is the author of ten books, mostly about living a chemical-free, old-fashioned life. She left the corporate world twenty years ago and now lives in the Hokianga with her husband, her father, twenty chickens (and counting), two cows, two dogs and three stray cats.